DATE DUE

The Business of Business

M. A. WRIGHT

Chairman of the Board
Humble Oil & Refining Company

The Business

With a Foreword by
ERWIN D. CANHAM

# of Business

PRIVATE ENTERPRISE AND PUBLIC AFFAIRS

 McGraw-Hill Book Company

NEW YORK   SAN FRANCISCO   TORONTO   LONDON   SYDNEY

*To Izetta and Judith,
for their encouragement,
interest, and support*

Foreword

The speeches which follow in this volume speak for themselves.

They show American business in its most responsible, its most intelligent, its most reasonable and balanced public posture.

They show the new American business executive. It is appropriate that they should come from a leader in the petroleum business, and that he should have been President of the Chamber of Commerce of the United States at a time when the public and the governmental relations of organized business were at a critical stage.

M. A. Wright brought to the U.S. Chamber the viewpoint of a lifelong engineer who must face facts, a Southwesterner who saw horizons as wide and hopeful, an executive in an immense, world-wide, progressively guided corporation. Thus he embodied attitudes which are particularly relevant to the American economy at this time.

These speeches, delivered during his year in office as President of the U.S. Chamber, cover an extraordinarily wide range. They are not negative speeches, fighting a desperate last-ditch fight against a powerful federal government. They are constructive speeches, emphasizing what business can do to help solve the problems government is tackling, and analyzing the pitfalls both for business and government.

Throughout, Mr. Wright urges business to be an active participant with government, not just a sniper at government. His credo was summarized in these words:

> If we want to preserve the principles of individual freedom and private initiative, we must devote an increasingly larger proportion of our time to meeting the nation's social needs. The day has passed when our public responsibility can be met merely by offering sideline criticism of the government's efforts. In effect, we must move into the social welfare field and offer constructive alternatives to the government's programs. At the same time, we must continue to encourage policies which will promote economic growth, still the greatest force in the fight against poverty.

Speaking as an oil man, he said: "The petroleum and auto industries cannot be satisfied until the automobile is made virtually smogless. This is an economically feasible goal and industry is working toward this end." But in this context he warned that if business did not move swiftly and effectively enough ". . . tomorrow our actions may be tightly controlled by government regulations." And he added this double-edged idea: "If our efforts in this area are made mandatory, not only will we be forced to take more costly and less efficient action, but we will also forfeit our claim to being a responsible segment of society."

The theme, then, is one of responsibility and of action and of common sense. It is a program which has great meaning not only to the United States, but to the world. If the "new economics" and the "new capitalism" can both be made to work in the United States, a powerful example will be set.

Mr. Wright takes an entirely sympathetic view toward the "new economics." He recognizes frankly the tremendous effect which governmental fiscal and monetary policies can have on the economy. He points out, however, that the old politics should not get in the way of the "new economics." He criticizes effectively the way in which government failed to use fiscal tools adequately to cool off the economy in 1966, thus putting inordinate burdens on monetary tools. But his quarrel is not with the "new economics" as such, merely with governmental irresponsibility and ineffectiveness and bad timing.

The "new capitalism" is illustrated by Mr. Wright's own overall viewpoint. He recognizes and avows great social responsibilities which all private business should manifest. His is a capitalism of stewardship, of social action, of responsiveness. It is a far cry from the capitalism of even twenty-five years ago. But it is the capitalism which helps make the American economy today fruitful, dynamic, and progressive in its use of new tools and its adoption of new attitudes.

The very absence of rhetorical flourish and emotionalism in these speeches is typical of the new attitudes. It is simple, straight talk. Mr. Wright has served well not only the U.S. Chamber but the cause of free competitive enterprise throughout the nation and the world by presenting this calm, lucid statement of its beliefs and commitments. Capitalists elsewhere can learn from these words that an acceptance of social duties is the best highway toward strength and indeed toward survival.

Erwin D. Canham
EDITOR IN CHIEF, *The Christian Science Monitor*
FORMERLY, PRESIDENT, Chamber of Commerce
of the United States

Contents

xi

*More active business participation in
public affairs is not only highly
desirable; it is an indispensable
function of effective business planning.*

1

Public Affairs: A Challenge
to the Business Community

Remarks before the Fifth Association Public Affairs Conference, Washington, D.C., February 2, 1967.

About 2,000 years ago, one of Athens' more astute citizens observed: "We do not say that a man who takes no interest in public affairs is a man who minds his own business. We say he has no business being here at all." This observation of Pericles is as appropriate and timely for modern America as it was for Ancient Greece.

The 1960s have been years of success and disappointments, years of milestones and paradox. We continue to enjoy the longest and most prosperous economic expansion in our nation's history; yet the responsiveness of our free market system faces persistent challenge. We have achieved the highest standard of living in the history of man; but at the same time, our concern over poverty and economic opportunity remains unusually acute. We have witnessed dramatic progress in the area of race equality; yet civil strife and disorder have grown to intense levels.

Embracing all these forces has been an emerging social consciousness; an awareness that the quality of man's life is as important as the quantity of his abundance; a recognition that some of America's greatest promises are yet to be fulfilled. Indeed we, as a nation and society, have become alert to the seemingly endless problems as well as great potentials of urbanization, industrialization, and internationalism.

All of these complex forces, as well as many others that can be recalled, have provided the impetus for ascendancy of the public sector. The demands and disappointments of society have spurred government to assume an ever-expanding role in society. Our daily lives have been increasingly affected by government policies and actions. No element of society remains untouched by this steadily growing force. The scope and magnitude of governmental influence have reached astounding proportions.

The government's influence is nowhere more evident than in the sphere of private business. Virtually every business decision today is affected by public laws, regulations, and policies. Wage and price practices face persistent government scrutiny; employment and personnel practices are tailored to government standards; and such business operations as product quality control, packaging, and advertising are gradually facing regulation from "the hill." In fact, the pervasiveness of governmental regulation recently caused George Champion of Chase Manhattan Bank to comment: "If anyone can find such a thing now as an 'unregulated industry,' he can sell it at a profit to the Smithsonian."

It was because of the successively larger role of government involvement in business and throughout the whole of America's economic and social structure that in 1962 the National Chamber of Commerce instituted public affairs conferences. At a time when government was setting more and more of the ground rules for business practices, when one of every six workers was employed by the public sector, and when one-fifth of the nation's output of goods and services was consumed by governmental units, there was a growing and urgent need to acquaint more businessmen with what was taking place in Washington. More active and enlightened business participation in public affairs was indeed not only highly desirable, but was fast becoming an indispensable function of effective business planning.

We had long realized that government involvement in business was a fact of life. We believed that it was overdue for business involvement in government to become an equally well-established fact of life. If our objective was worthwhile five years ago, and I think it was, it is surely even more important today.

Looking back over recent years, it seems obvious that the business community's interest in governmental activities and decisions is on an upward trend. And in most respects, this growing involvement has been well received in government circles. We have in fact, to a limited degree, become trusted consultants to various government agencies. There are now 33 official government commissions and boards on which businessmen sit. These groups advise Congress and the executive branch on such diverse and important subjects as the balance of payments, civil rights, and emergency mobilization.

Despite our expanding role in directing and formulating public policy, however, I fear our past efforts have been neither sufficient nor as effective as they could have been. Our success in dealing with the government has frequently been tempered by outdated views or politically naïve approaches. We have too often diminished our impact by failing to offer positive alternatives to government programs. We have indeed, at times, frustrated our common objectives by promoting a disunified and inconsistent business front. For these reasons, we should briefly reflect on how our public affairs role can be made more positive and more effective.

We should begin, I believe, by encouraging more meetings where businessmen are brought face to face with public officials and are able to discuss in complete candor the problems and issues of the day. We can act responsibly in the area of public policy only if we are well informed on government programs and legislative proposals. Our effectiveness can surely be no greater than our knowledge and understanding of the relevant issues. A businessman's daily education must include as much emphasis on legislative trends and developments in Washington as on the latest production or marketing techniques.

Our effectiveness in public affairs can also be improved by presenting a more positive response to government actions. All too often it is said that when we react to a legislative proposal or a new program, we are against it. Instead of trying to improve the proposal or program—or even better to offer a constructive alternative to it—we offer nothing more than criticism of what was proposed.

As a consequence of this typical response—or at least what too many people believe to be our typical response—some government officials and far too many other segments of society have a stereotyped image of business. They presume that if a businessman participates in public affairs, he is attempting to slow down and destroy some program, rather than perhaps to improve its efficiency or enhance its effectiveness. It is even possible that our image has caused government to sometimes assume our reaction to a given proposal or program in advance, and thus reduce our opportunities to make constructive suggestions on vital issues.

As a possible means of removing this negative—or sometimes at best, passive—image, I have been encouraged by the recent emergence of business participation in programs traditionally reserved for government. In my opinion, a great number of public programs could be carried out with greater efficiency by the private sector. Business activity in such areas as manpower training, urban renewal, pollution abatement, and many others could not only reduce the seriousness of many social problems, but could also in the long run prove profitable for private enterprise. I would hope that in the future more businessmen will search out areas where they can offer the nation a constructive alternative, thus reasserting our image as a positive force in society.

This year we should have a good opportunity to put our best foot forward, to be creative instead of indifferent, to be positive instead of negative. Where we believe we can do something better than government can, we should say so. Where we believe the government can do something better and more efficiently, it is our responsibility to speak out in the interest of society. To say that we would rather not get involved is to deny reality. We *are* involved. We must realize that government, and particularly good government, is the responsibility of all citizens. And business is certainly one of the nation's most important and influential citizens. Once government and the public know that we accept our responsibilities, we can have a greater voice in shaping the nation's economic and political climate.

A further method of enhancing our effectiveness in public affairs is for business to provide a more unified response to public policies. We too often subordinate the common good to our own sectional and industrial interests. We ignore legislation, or at least fail to offer a reasoned response, when the proposed action is not directly related to our own business endeavors. This in effect causes us to focus on the immediate problem at the expense of guiding and influencing more general long-term trends.

The business community has many interests in common, and we must recognize that these interests are best defended by a united effort. I am not suggesting that the businessman can afford to ease up in waging his own industry's or company's battles. Without these efforts there would be a real breach in the ranks. My point is that as government programs become more extensive, there must be more togetherness on the business side, as we provide a broader, more enlightened response to decisions in the public sector.

 Finally, I believe business can improve its public affairs role by assuming even greater responsibilities at the state and local levels. Many federal programs could be more efficiently handled by people and agencies at the local level. But because businessmen—and many of their fellow citizens—have failed to respond to local issues and problems, federal government has been forced to move in and attempt to solve these ills. If this trend is to be reversed, enlightened business leaders must help make state and local agencies more effective tools of social progress.

These are only four ways that I find attractive for improving the role of business in public affairs. I am sure there are many others. We as businessmen have an important role to perform in this modern and dynamic society. Governments at all levels need our help, and there is no reason why businessmen should not contribute to the forces that mold our society. No element has more at stake in the outcome than the business community. We must devise better approaches to many of the existing public programs. The urgency of this endeavor demands the same energy and imagination that we apply to the operations of our own businesses. Many problems lie ahead, but we have the opportunity, indeed the responsibility, to help formulate the best solutions.

As we pinpoint those areas where we can make the greatest contribution, we can detect areas in which government action is needed and others where present action is inefficient. This is an exercise in public responsibility. It involves economic understanding—knowing how to size up the problem in its relation to business and society; it involves political participation—making your voice heard in the political arena; and finally, it involves legislative action—advising government on what can and should be done. The success of the total effort, however, must depend on how well you carry out your responsibilities as a good citizen and an enlightened businessman.

*If American businessmen want to preserve
the principles of individual freedom and
private initiative, they must devote an
increasingly larger proportion of their
time to meeting the nation's social needs.*

2

*Private Enterprise
and the Great Society*

Speech before the Chicago Association of Commerce and Industry, Chicago. Illinois, July 28, 1966.

The nation's social needs are numerous and complex. However, I would like to center our attention on one of the oldest and most persistent of our social problems—economic poverty. It is poverty that stands as the biggest obstacle on the road to the kind of society that we all want.

To help place this problem in its proper setting, I would like to begin by taking a look at the overall economic wellbeing of the people in the United States. By doing this, we can help define the issues and perhaps eliminate some of the misconceptions.

We might note, first of all, that the average household income in the United States today is approximately $7,000. If postwar growth rates continue, by the year 2000 the average American family will be earning an annual income of about $20,000 in today's dollars. These figures represent the attainment of an economic abundance never before dreamed of.

Unfortunately, all Americans are not participating in the nation's prosperity and economic progress. Though the unemployment rate for white workers averaged about 4 percent in 1965, the rate for non-white workers was above 8 percent. Certain minority groups, teenagers, and the poorly educated or poorly trained faced even greater employment difficulties.

As recently as March of 1966, in the midst of one of the longest booms in history, there were still about 32 million Americans in families earning less than $3,000 a year. An additional 16 million Americans depended on a family income of between $3,000 and $4,000 annually. Within these low-income families, the incidence of poverty falls disproportionately heavily on certain groups.

Admittedly, poverty is a relative term, but using the government's current definition, the Office of Economic Opportunity estimates that more than 50 percent of Negro families in the United States are poor, compared with less than 15 percent of all whites. About one-fourth of the people living in rural areas are poor, compared with only 14 percent of those living in urban areas. Poverty among families headed by women is three times more prevalent than that among families headed by men, and more than one-fourth of the aged are poor.

Yet the social cost of poverty is not fully measured by these statistics or the privation they suggest. Today, in varying degrees, the desperation and frustration that result from poverty contribute to ill health, to deteriorating citizenship values, and to other factors that weaken society. The social cost of poverty must also include the goods and services that are not produced because of the unemployment and low productivity of the poor.

At the same time, however, we should recognize that although large numbers are classified as poor by government definitions, very few Americans today are actually denied the minimum acceptable level of health, housing, food, and education. In 1960, only about 7 percent of American dwelling units were dilapidated. By 1964, more than 90 percent of American households had television. Four out of every five households had telephones and at least one automobile.

Among families earning $3,000 or less, even the poor enjoy more material well-being than might be thought. For example, over 75 percent own a television set, about half have both a television set and a telephone, three-fourths own a washing machine, 20 percent own a home freezer, and 65 percent have a dwelling unit that is not dilapidated, with running water and bathroom facilities for their own use. In 1965, approximately one in seven bought a car.

Moreover, some important strides have been made in eliminating poverty. A 1965 report revealed that "with a fixed definition of poverty, in real terms, poverty declined three-fourths of the way toward total elimination between 1929 and 1962." Even during the relatively short span of the current expansion, Professor Otto Eckstein of Harvard University says that "the number of persons and families below the poverty line has diminished by seven million, from over 22 percent to less than 17 percent of all Americans." Indeed, the single greatest force in the battle against poverty continues to be sustained economic growth.

My purpose in citing these figures is not to minimize our poverty problems. Rather, it is hoped that these statistics will help us see the nation's needs in a more accurate perspective than is possible under the emotional atmosphere that often pervades discussions of this subject. It is also hoped that these figures show that as our economy has grown, considerable progress has already been made in eliminating poverty from the national scene.

Of equal importance, however, is that these statistics point out the relative nature of poverty. Though only a small minority of Americans actually suffers from inadequate food, clothing, or shelter, there is still a portion of society that has not participated fully in the American dream of a good life—or, more important, a satisfying life. Freedom from want is more than freedom from hunger and exposure—it is being allowed the opportunity of earning a decent living, of enjoying economic security, and of recognizing one's potential. To be meaningful, freedom from want must include hope—hope for a better life and a more fulfilling life.

It is this last element—hope for a better life—that continues to elude many of America's poor. Knowing nothing but the cycle of poverty—a cycle extending back for generations in some cases—far too many of the poor have little incentive for expecting a better life, or for that matter, going out and working for a better life. Their employment opportunities have usually been marginal at best and often nonexistent. More than 60 percent are unskilled and about 80 percent did not complete high school. In most cases, their poverty appears to be a natural outgrowth of low education, low skill, and low motivation.

In recent years, the federal government has taken on much of the responsibility for eliminating poverty and for solving the nation's other social problems. For example, the Department of Health, Education and Welfare is scheduled to spend almost $12 billion in 1967 on social needs, an increase of 33 percent over the 1965 appropriations and a 485 percent gain over HEW's first budget in 1953. In addition, the Office of Economic Opportunity has, in less than two years, spent more than $2 billion on its much publicized "War on Poverty." For fiscal year 1967 alone, this agency's antipoverty budget is expected to be about $2 billion, and even larger appropriations can be anticipated in future years.

The Commerce Department's Appalachian Regional Development Program, which was started in 1965, will spend over a billion dollars during a five-year period in the hope of reviving one of the nation's most seriously afflicted areas. Under provisions of the Public Works and Economic Development Act of 1965, such regions as New England, the Ozarks, the upper Midwest, and still others are prepared to follow the route of Appalachia.

These outlays, large as they are, reflect only a small part of the tremendous commitments envisioned for the future. The National Planning Association estimates that by 1975, all levels of government will spend about $85 billion annually for welfare payments, health, education, and job preparation. This is almost twice the amount spent in 1965 on these social needs.

These figures do not include the latest and perhaps most controversial welfare proposal. Just a few weeks ago, a congressionally created task force proposed that all Americans should be guaranteed a minimum level of income and social services as a matter of legal right. The chairman of the task force estimated that adopting this proposal would increase the annual bill for federal–state–local public assistance payments from the present $6 billion to about $15 billion a year.

Expenditures of this magnitude call for careful consideration. I think many questions must be answered before the American public can fully support the Great Society approach to solving the nation's social problems. For instance, does the situation merit or necessitate such large expenditures by the federal government? Are there better solutions than large-scale government welfare programs? Are the government's expenditures being channeled in the right direction, or do they deter and destroy individual initiative, thus further aggravating the problem?

The objective of satisfying the nation's social needs and eliminating poverty commends itself to all Americans. But so far, many of the government's efforts to achieve this objective have left much to be desired. Far too often political expediency has taken precedence over economic effectiveness. Poorly thought-out proposals and expensive stopgap measures have been accepted when more carefully planned programs could have achieved greater results at a lower cost to the taxpayer.

For example, the Appalachian Regional Development Act —often cited as an antipoverty measure—sets aside 80 percent of its authorized $1 billion-plus for the construction of roads. This comes when studies show that Appalachia could use more than 100 additional vocational training schools. Is it not likely that expenditures on education and job training would yield greater benefits for the Appalachian poor and the nation than a massive road-building program which, for the most part, creates only temporary employment, much of which goes to skilled workmen from outside the area?

Many of the War on Poverty programs raise similar questions. In terms of number of participants, the Neighborhood Youth Corps is the largest human development project currently in operation. Yet the program has not been primarily geared to train people for the private, profit-making economy where most jobs and opportunities exist. Instead, the law restricts employment of Youth Corps members to public or nonprofit organizations and facilities. Here is an open invitation for make-work projects, perhaps leading to poor work habits and misdirected incentives.

Although the intended purpose of the Job Corps is laudable—transforming unemployed and unemployable youths into productive citizens—the expense and effectiveness of this program must be questioned. According to some estimates, the cost of training a corpsman for one year runs as high as $11,000; and though the program has been operating for two years, only about 40 percent of the 6,000-plus graduates have received jobs or have gone into the armed services or back to school. This low placement ratio suggests that there may be a more effective and less costly method of training these young people than is currently offered by the Job Corps.

A criticism of these specific programs, however, does not sufficiently point up the deficiencies of the War on Poverty. The greatest shortcoming of this massive campaign seems to be that inadequate thought has gone into formulating its plans and policies. In May of 1966, according to the *Washington Post,* a confidential White House task force implied that the effectiveness of antipoverty programs was in jeopardy because key decisions had been avoided. Among other things, it was revealed that even though the antipoverty effort had been operational for two years, the Office of Economic Opportunity had not yet clearly defined the exact purpose or policy of many programs.

These are only a few examples of the problems attending government efforts to meet the nation's social needs, but they serve to illustrate the necessity for the business community to become even more aware of the nation's social issues and to become more involved in helping solve these problems. Businessmen must assume more of a leading role in the nation's fight against social ills, or a habit-forming dependence on the federal government could well undermine our traditional concepts of personal initiative, individual freedom, and private enterprise.

The business community's involvement with social problems must, in other words, take on a new look. Businessmen can no longer afford to restrict their efforts to supplying money and criticism. In the search for solutions to these problems, they must bring into play their leadership and their analytical capabilities. They must help devise new and better approaches to the existing public programs. In short, businessmen have no practical choice but to insist that social problems be given the same careful analytical treatment that business uses in solving its own problems.

I am optimistic that businessmen will accept their public responsibility and offer imaginative solutions to the nation's problems. And there are good reasons for such optimism. The advance of technology has seen management education shift from a narrow professional or vocational base to deeper study of technical fields, the scientific method, and the content of the social sciences.

Today's businessmen realize that our success in coming this far toward the elimination of poverty attests to the stamina and ingenuity of the competitive system and of the men who guide its activities. But they also realize that we must now devote the same knowledge and ability, not only to making life more affluent, but also to making it more satisfying and rewarding.

In pursuing this objective, businessmen should become increasingly involved in what can be called the "strategy of the constructive alternative." In response to "creative federalism," it can offer in many areas "creative competition" between business and government to serve the national interest. George Champion of the Chase Manhattan Bank, put it this way: "Just imagine," he said, "what could be accomplished if some of [our] competitive zest were channeled into public service. Think of the good that could be done if business were to launch an all-out campaign of creative competition with government in developing imaginative new approaches to economic and social problems."

This leads me to the main point which I want to make. Creative competition offers businessmen a way of becoming involved in social welfare programs at the corporate, local, and national levels. Corporate involvement has already become a successful reality in many cases. During 1965, for instance, one of the nation's largest manufacturers of building materials initiated its own urban development program in the Harlem slums of New York. Instead of waiting for government agencies to move in, dislocate the families, raze the buildings, and then rebuild tenement apartments at taxpayer expense, this private enterpriser has taken over a block of Harlem slums and shown how they can be renovated by private initiative. Preliminary cost data show that the dwellings can be completely refurbished for about $9,000 per unit, less than half the unit cost for urban renewal housing.

Another excellent example of business commitment to social progress at the local level is found in the work of the Chicago Association of Commerce and Industry. In your own antipoverty effort, you have attempted to reduce illiteracy among welfare recipients, thus allowing them the opportunity to become self-supporting. You have taken a positive stand on the need for further community redevelopment programs and more low-cost housing for the poor. Perhaps of even greater significance have been your merit employment activities. Realizing that much more must be done in providing job opportunities for minority groups, you have sought the help of all businessmen in providing employment without regard to race, creed, or color. In recognition of these efforts and those of your fellow citizens, a national magazine some weeks ago said, "More than most big towns, broad-shouldered Chicago is mobilized for civic responsibility."

Other cities are also taking affirmative action to ameliorate what has been called the pathology of poverty. In 1964, for example, the Philadelphia Negro community with the support of the local Chamber initiated its own private job training and employment program. In less than two years, some 1,500 potentially unemployable persons have been placed in productive positions, most of which are classified as semiskilled or skilled. In Newark, New Jersey, several local businesses—my own company among them—have joined in a program which encourages high school dropouts to resume their education and also places them in jobs at the same time. This program is now in its third year of operation, and it has so far obtained permanent jobs for 70 percent of the dropouts.

At the national level, an excellent example of how businessmen can participate in social welfare issues is the National Chamber's Task Force on Economic Growth and Opportunity. This is a group of more than 100 chief executives of American corporations which is making extensive studies of major domestic social and economic problems. For two years, the Task Force has devoted its efforts to a study of poverty. Thirty-seven experts have been commissioned to develop background papers on this problem, and some 150 other authorities have been consulted. The studies completed so far have proved very useful to government and academic leaders as well as to the business community. Now the Task Force is moving into a similar study of urban problems.

Further examples of business action on social problems at the national level are found in the work of the Committee for Economic Development, the National Industrial Conference Board, and the National Association of Manufacturers. The CED and NICB have for many years held scholarly conferences and discussions on public issues with a view to making businessmen aware of the work that must be done. The NAM currently trains school dropouts for productive jobs, seeks to help its member companies solve manpower development problems, and is helping businessmen measure up to their full public responsibility.

Our nation is approaching a significant milestone in history. The nation's social conscience calls for a dedicated and continuing effort to help all our citizens achieve a better way of life.

Recently, the federal government has assumed the initiative in eradicating poverty. Unfortunately, however, many of its efforts appear to have been ineffective and overly costly. It is imperative, therefore, that business leaders throughout the country become more involved at the corporate, local, and national levels in solving the nation's social problems.

If we want to preserve the principles of individual freedom and private initiative, we must devote an increasingly larger proportion of our time to meeting the nation's social needs. The day has passed when our public responsibility can be met merely by offering sideline criticism of the government's efforts. In effect, we must move into the social welfare field and offer constructive alternatives to the government's programs. At the same time, we must continue to encourage policies which will promote economic growth, still the greatest force in the fight against poverty.

If businessmen hope to merit a central position in our society, we must work at helping solve society's social problems with the same energy and imagination that we apply to the nation's economic problems. This challenge demands the best of every American business leader.

The pollution problem is a troublesome by-product of progress. All segments of society have created the problem, and all segments will have to be parties to the solution.

3

Air and Water: A Time for Decision

Speech before the Houston Chamber of Commerce, Houston, Texas, December 6, 1966.

Concern over the quality of the air we breathe and the water we drink has become a public issue of the first magnitude. But like many issues facing society, it is widely misunderstood and susceptible to varying degrees of emotion, alarm, ignorance, and indifference.

Contamination of air and water dates from the beginning of time. Unpleasant and even poisonous substances found their way into our air and water long before man became an accomplished polluter. Even before the spread of civilization, forest fires, dust storms, and volcanic eruptions poured vast quantities of contaminants into the air. To the great discomfort of those with allergy problems, plants have been contaminating the air with pollen for hundreds of centuries. In fact, one of the conditions for the earth's existence has been some degree of pollution.

Nor is man-made pollution something peculiar to the 20th century. It has only become more highly developed in our time. Untold generations of mankind have dumped trash and wastes into our streams. Smoke and soot have contaminated the air ever since Stone Age man first began building fires in unventilated caves. Residents of Ancient Rome complained that airborne soot smudged their wool garments. London in 1660 was described as having "her stately head in clouds of smoke and sulphur."

The Industrial Revolution, however, created new problems and stepped up the contamination process. Along with its new-found wealth came the odors and unsightliness of industrial

27

wastes and factory smokestacks. While industrialization raised man's standard of living, it lowered the quality of his most vital resources—air and water. Now, some hundred years later, it appears that the quality of these resources may be significantly affected merely by living in the manner to which we have become accustomed.

The full extent of America's pollution problem defies accurate measurement. It is increasingly obvious, however, that we have a serious problem on our hands, and one that seems to be growing more serious each year. Though I cannot agree with those who fear that we will be destroyed by our own environment, there are too many locations in the United States where the air or water has become objectionable, unpleasant, and— on occasions—a hazard.

Man's potential for damaging his environment is continually increasing. The U.S. Public Health Service estimates that we Americans, in performing our normal activities, release some 360,000 tons of principal pollutants into the atmosphere each day. We also produce nearly 400,000 tons of waste material each day. Enough of this flows into our lakes and rivers to jeopardize their usefulness for recreation or consumption purposes. Secretary of the Interior Udall recently warned that, in the absence of effective remedial action, parts of the Great Lakes are threatened with an early and unnatural death. And according to New York's Governor Rockefeller, sections of the Hudson River are so contaminated that fish are unable to live in them.

In its most simple terms, pollution results from the daily activities of an increasing number of people. In 1900, some three million square miles of the United States accommodated the daily activities of less than 80 million people. Today, that same area—and the same amount of air and water—must accommodate the activities of nearly 200 million people.

Moreover, at the turn of the century our nation was predominantly rural; today it is predominantly urban. In 1900, less than one person in three lived in a major metropolitan area. Today two-thirds of our population live in urban areas, and according to one source, 85 percent of the people live on less than 2 percent of the land.

Pollution is also in many respects an offshoot of progress. As our nation has become more highly mechanized, our ability to contaminate our environment has steadily increased. In 1900, for example, the nation's car population was almost nil. Today it is over 70 million and is projected to approach 120 million by 1980. Not even the boldest of forecasters project this trend to the year 2000.

A hundred years ago, isolation of the sources of air and water pollution was a simpler matter. One could merely point to an industrial smokestack or trace the scum on the water to a manufacturing plant's waste outlet and the question was answered. There was the prime polluter—industry.

Today, however, assigning the responsibility for air and water pollution is not that simple. Although industry still receives most of the blame, it has in recent years become less and less the main offender. In defining the causes of air pollution, a recent report by the National Academy of Sciences said that less than one-third of the principal atmospheric pollutants released in the U.S. comes from manufacturing plants or electricity-generating complexes. The remaining two-thirds come from other sources, mainly individuals and municipalities.

Even in the area of water pollution, where industry continues to be depicted as the main culprit, recent studies indicate that community sewage is an equal and oftentimes greater de-spoiler of our waterways. Murray Stein, Federal Commissioner for Water Pollution Control, has said that "the underlying cause of water pollution is that all over the country you have municipal sewage systems that are inadequate for the loads that have been imposed on them in the last few years."

The fact is that the problem of air and water contamination involves all of modern society. Pollutants are released whenever backyard leaves are burned, whenever an automobile is used, whenever apartment or municipal trash is incinerated, wherever inadequate city sewage treatment facilities discharge wastes into rivers. One study early this year revealed that in New York City alone several hundred thousand tons per day of sewage remain untreated, and the city's 11 municipal incinerators contribute more than 35 tons of objectionable matter to the atmosphere each day. In Houston, according to one newspaper, the city's own sewage plants have on occasion been singled out as serious offenders. In short, all segments of society have created the pollution problem, and all segments will now have to be parties to the solution.

The best solution to the problem of restoring and maintaining the quality of our air and water lies in a well-coordinated, communitywide effort. No single segment of society is capable of accomplishing the job that lies ahead. But as in the case of all community programs, some group must take the initiative in getting an effective program underway. In my opinion, this group should be the community's business leaders. If a reasoned and reasonable response to this growing problem is to be forthcoming, business leadership must play an active and consistent role.

I am not suggesting that businessmen have ignored their social responsibility in connection with this problem. This is true of some, but others have made substantial contributions toward improving the quality of air and water. In just the last 10 years, for example, the electric power industry has spent some $750 million dollars on air and water conservation. Over the same period, the chemical and petroleum industries have spent a similar amount on pollution control equipment, and are now spending additional millions of dollars a year to operate, improve, and expand this equipment. In all its operations this year, the petroleum industry will spend more than $10 million just on air and water conservation research with the aim of making its future efforts even more effective than those of the past.

Industry is also making strides toward reducing the polluting capacity of its products. The automobile, for instance, is commonly assigned much of the responsibility for urban smog. For example, Health, Education and Welfare Secretary John Gardner has said that the automobile may be on a "collision course" with pressures for clean air. Other officials have suggested that the pollution problem can be solved only by outlawing the gasoline engine and replacing it with a non-polluting propulsion system.

The concern expressed by Secretary Gardner and other officials is shared by the public. This concern, however, results in part from industry's failure to acquaint the public with the progress modern technology is making in reducing automobile emissions. A few years ago the auto makers devised a crank case ventilation system which, according to Governor Brown of California, has reduced smog in that state by at least

10 percent. In 1968, all new cars will be equipped with a device that will substantially reduce exhaust contaminants. Other contributions in the quest for a pollution-free engine will be forthcoming. One of these promises to virtually eliminate all evaporative losses from an automobile's carburetor and gas tank.

Additional progress, however, can and should be made. The automobile and its current form of propulsion is a direct response to the needs and desires of the American people. From the available estimates, no alternative form of power can satisfy the requirements of our society at such a low cost. Hence, if the American public is to continue enjoying flexible and economical transportation, and still satisfy its desire for cleaner air, the petroleum and auto industries cannot be satisfied until the automobile is made virtually smogless. This is an economically feasible goal and industry is working toward this end.

But industry must not only do more to reduce the polluting capacity of its products. It must also reduce the contaminants from its plants and other operations. Many industrial firms still refuse to take appropriate antipollution action, if any action at all. They seem convinced that the problem is perhaps not serious, or that it will in time solve itself. Such individuals seem to have an abiding faith in the compensating ability of nature, or seem to believe that if everyone else took effective measures, they would not need to act. The evidence suggests that such blind faith is not justified. If this problem is to be solved, all business concerns, large and small, must do their share.

I cannot overemphasize the challenge which pollution presents to business leaders. If our efforts to resolve this problem fail to merit the confidence of the public, the Auto Safety Act of 1966 could well be the prelude to the "Pollution Control Act" of 1967.

We in business have only two alternatives. Either we voluntarily implement effective pollution abatement programs—at all levels of business and industry—or in the near future our actions in this area will be spelled out by congressional legislation. Today, we still have the freedom to make a reasoned and resolute response to the problem; tomorrow our actions may be tightly controlled by government regulations. If our efforts in this area are made mandatory, not only will we be forced to take more costly and less efficient action, but also we will forfeit our claim to being a responsible segment of society. To those who say they cannot afford to take effective antipollution measures, I can only respond that they can't afford not to.

Business alone, however, cannot restore and maintain America's environmental heritage. Government must also make its contribution. Efforts in the private sector must be supplemented, and in some cases coordinated, by sound antipollution programs on the part of government. With the advice and support of knowledgeable business leaders, the local and state authorities should formulate reasonable community goals and the programs which are needed to achieve these goals. Business can also help establish communitywide pollution standards and requirements that are feasible and work to see that the public officials have the support and authority to enforce them.

From the available evidence, there is room for improvement in the efforts of our municipal and state governments. The

Public Health Service estimates that some 7,300 communities are affected by air pollution, but only 130 cities, counties, or regions have established antipollution programs. Many of these are judged by the Health Service to be grossly inadequate. More than 2,000 American communities pour untreated sewage into the nation's lakes and rivers. An additional 700 municipalities in the United States have sewer systems with inadequate refuse-treatment facilities. Fewer than half our states have air pollution laws on their books, and most of these are of the antiquated "smoke law" variety.

If the pollution problem is to be solved, and it must be, it is imperative that more state and local governments play an active role. In most cases, the problem is a local responsibility, and we should see that it remains such. But if effective local programs are not implemented, we may be assured that federal action will be forthcoming. It behooves all of us—local officials, industry, and interested citizens—to take the appropriate remedial action and accept our proper responsibility.

The final responsibility of effective business leadership is to educate the public as to what can be done and how much it will cost. Here again, I believe business has been negligent. Society must be made fully aware that though the prospect of clean, country air and water in the city is pleasant, the cost of achieving this goal may be prohibitive. Society must realize that to achieve this level of clean air and water involves more than just having industry spend money on crash programs.

The average citizen, for example, would have to buy add-on exhaust controls for his car. He would have to pay for at least annual testing to ensure their efficient operation. He would be required to pay additional taxes so the city could purchase smoke-free incinerators and vastly improved facilities for the treatment of sewage. He would be forced to collect the leaves in his yard and pay for an inspection system which assures that he doesn't burn them. In some parts of the country his office space or apartment rent might also have to be boosted because of higher electrical costs and higher heating costs resulting from more expensive low-sulfur fuel.

The public must realize that, in the final analysis, the problem of air and water pollution is closely linked to economics. The purity of our air and water depends almost entirely on how much we are willing to pay. Senator Muskie of Maine, chairman of the Subcommittee on Air and Water Pollution, believes that $100 billion will be required by the year 2000 just to clean up the waterways. A recent article in the *Harvard Business Review* estimated that total expenditures of at least $275 billion will be required over the next 34 years to ensure the availability of clean air and water. Of this sum, $110 billion will be needed to control and reverse water pollution, $105 billion to abate and control air pollution, and $60 billion for disposing of wastes.

An informed and enlightened public must realize that outlays of this magnitude will be necessary to satisfy its desires for a relatively pollution-free environment. The public must also understand that a large part of this sum will come directly from its own pockets. When these facts are widely known, society can than make the necessary judgments on how clean it wants air and water to be. We can achieve almost any desired level of purity, but we must be willing to pay the price.

Given complete information, the community will probably decide on a course of action somewhere between the extreme positions. The one extreme is that no price is too great to restore our air and water to their natural purity. The other extreme is that no pollution problem actually exists. The first position would result in a waste of capital and would jeopardize future progress. The second position would result in the waste of our two most essential resources. Industry, government, and the individual must decide, on the basis of costs and benefits, what level of purity they wish to attain.

No reasonable person would suggest that man not use his environment or that he revert to his primitive past. But at the same time no reasonable person can condone the misuse of two resources needed to sustain life.

Society must come to grips with the problem of air and water conservation. We must not do this, however, in a mood of panic. We must develop a reasoned and effective response to the challenge. To be specific, industry must act responsibly, government must act fairly, the public must act with understanding. The time for decision is here.

With technology expanding at an explosive rate, the nation's educational system must prepare to cope with challenges far more complex and urgent than those of the past.

4

Education, Business, and the Future

Speech before the student body of Shaw University, Raleigh, North Carolina, February 13, 1967.

By almost any measure, the 20th century has been a time of dynamic technological and economic change. Since the turn of the century, we have witnessed a 200-fold increase in the speed at which man can travel. Over the same time span, such breakthroughs as radio, television, and the communications satellite have revolutionized man's ability to communicate. Advances in such fields as medicine, psychology, and chemistry, to name but a few, have been so striking as to defy the comprehension of the average layman. And the development of nuclear energy has placed at man's disposal a source of power which could result in either unlimited good or immeasurable harm.

These developments have been accompanied by substantial advances in economic welfare. Since 1914, the average weekly earnings of our workers have increased from about $10 a week to almost $110 a week. At the same time, the leisure of America's workers has been enhanced by a 20 percent cut in the average work week. And even after allowing for price changes and tax increases—which have been substantial—the real income of our labor force has increased some threefold. In the relatively short period of 20 years, real output in the United States has doubled, and real disposable income per person has grown about one-half.

Because of this rapid growth, the United States is by far the most prosperous nation in the world. With only 7 percent of the world's population and 6 percent of its land area, we currently produce about one-third of the world's total output. In fact, the annual *increase* in our output of goods and services is larger than the *total output* of all but a few other nations in the world.

With these past achievements as prologue, we are understandably anticipating even more dramatic progress in the future. And for the most part, these anticipations seem fully justified. Today, there are about 400,000 scientists in the United States, more than triple the number of just 20 years ago. It is estimated, in fact, that of all the scientists who ever lived, 90 percent are alive today. To support this large and growing number of scientists, our nation will commit $25 billion this year to research and development, some three times the amount spent just 10 years ago.

It is thus reasonable to expect this increasing emphasis on science and research to accelerate technological change. One recent study has shown this to be true. Before World War I the typical time lag between a scientific or engineering discovery and recognition of its commercial potential was about 30 years. Between the wars this lag declined by about one-half, and in the post-World War II period, the time between a technical discovery and its application has been about nine years. Recent developments in the fields of electronics, computer and space technologies, and many others suggest this lag has been even further reduced in the past few years.

Technological innovation gives birth to new and better products and allows us to produce existing products more efficiently. Thus, acceleration of scientific development certainly bodes well for the future. Indeed, predictions about the approaching age of abundance, of leisure, and of a host of new and exotic goods and services are enough to make us envy the next generation. Economists tell us that with even modest success, the nation's output in today's prices will exceed $1 trillion in 1975. Further, they see the classic income pyramid being inverted in the next decade, as fewer people earn low incomes and an increasingly larger proportion of the population is concentrated in the $15,000-and-over income range.

The strength and vitality of the nation's economic system and our growing commitment to science and technology seem to make these favorable expectations well founded. Yet, we must not let our optimism make us careless and nearsighted, perhaps blinding us to the very pitfalls which could slow or even prevent these bright prospects. It would certainly be foolish, and costly, to take unlimited progress for granted. As in the past, there will be many impediments and barriers which must be overcome if the nation is to fully realize its great promise. We must be fully as alert to the potential problems as to the potential progress if the future is to be as rewarding as we all hope.

The challenges and problems will be nowhere more acute than in our educational complex. The success of the future—as the success of the past—will in large measure be determined by the responsiveness and imagination of the nation's educational system. In a society that will become increasingly more complex—and undergo change at an even faster pace—a person's education will determine not only his livelihood but indeed the very essence of the life he leads. If the educational system meets the demands that will be placed upon it, many changes will be forthcoming.

The most urgent demand placed upon tomorrow's educators will be to keep abreast of the very knowledge explosion that they themselves have helped create. Technology, for example, has advanced more in the last 50 years—if in fact not more in the last 15 years—than in all the previous history of mankind. It is estimated that man's total knowledge will double over the next 10 years. Another source estimates that there is roughly 100 times as much to know today as there was in 1900, and there will probably be 1,000 times as much to be learned by the end of the century. It is no doubt startling to realize that most of the knowledge today's student will need in his lifetime has not yet been discovered, and much of what he has already learned will soon be obsolete or irrelevant.

In its most simple terms, the educational system of tomorrow will be faced with the task of providing more knowledge in less time to more people. With scientific discovery and technological change continuing apace, man's control and mastery of his environment will be determined by his store of knowledge and the wisdom with which he uses it. The future of mankind, H. G. Wells once said, depends on the outcome of a race between education and catastrophe. There is certainly no more urgent challenge than to see that this race is won by education.

If our educational system is to measure up to the task at hand, the first requisite is a more receptive attitude among teachers and administrators toward new and better techniques of teaching and learning. Ironically, such an attitude has often been absent in the past. In fact, education—which has been a prime mover in the technological and scientific revolution of the 20th century—has remained almost untouched by change in its own operations. While almost every other institution has witnessed rapid innovations and improvements in recent years, the methods and equipment used in preparing the nation's most valuable resource—human intelligence—have remained nearly unchanged.

Perhaps one of the most notable examples of education's slow response to change has been its inadequate—and in most cases nonexistent—use of computers and computer technology in both administration and in teaching. Business has long realized the tremendous benefits of computers for purposes as diverse as data collection and filing to the development of mathematical models for optimization and simulation purposes. Computers have revolutionized such business functions as inventory control, investment policies, and distribution practices. A modern computer can perform more calculations in one hour than a football stadium full of scientists could in a lifetime. As a result, the cost of making one million calculations has declined from $30,000 in precomputer days to about 30 cents today.

In the hands of imaginative teachers and administrators, computerized teaching devices could cause equally dramatic and revolutionary changes in the educational process. Through the use of programmed learning—which is not nearly so depersonalized as it may sound—the possibilities of individualized training are unlimited. By allowing each student to pursue a course of study at a pace set by his own capabilities, rather than at a norm set for a large group of students with dissimilar attributes, all our young people would have a better opportunity to realize their full intellectual potential. By eliminating memory work, the computer would allow the student more time to think and to analyze problems, thus making him more capable of understanding and mastering the knowledge that he acquires. In addition, our teachers would be allowed more free time for individual instruction and discussion. With many of their routine functions removed, teachers would also have a greater opportunity for the creative and resourceful effort necessary to improve the whole of a student's educational experience.

The computer is only one of many technological developments that can be applied to the teaching process. There are many others—such as closed circuit TV systems, electronic teaching machines, centralized tape libraries—that will no doubt offer equally promising results. It will behoove all of us to see that tomorrow's educators have the most advanced teaching techniques available. If tomorrow's student is to be adequately prepared for his place in our space age society, our methods of learning must be as highly developed as the electronic circuitry of the space ship he will travel in.

But rapid and imaginative changes in the techniques of teaching and learning will not be the only change required of the educational complex of the future. If the nation is to realize its full promise, tomorrow's educators must be equally as sensitive to changes in the substance and purpose of education as to the techniques by which it is taught. Unless the abilities and skills that are developed in the classroom are those which are demanded by the nation's economic and social institutions, the techniques and methods used—or even the rapidity of the learning process—will not be pertinent.

Our future progress could, in fact, be seriously constrained should a more serious imbalance develop between the skills and professions needed by our economy and those actually possessed by the labor force. As economic and technological changes become not only more complex, but also occur at an accelerated rate, the need for a perceptive and responsive educational institution will become even more critical.

It has been predicted that in 1975, some three-fourths of our labor force will be producing goods and services that have not yet been developed. Unless educators—and other public and private policymakers—demonstrate unusually keen foresight, our future economic and technological achievements could be tarnished by a large and growing reserve of inadequately or inappropriately prepared workers.

The Bureau of Labor Statistics, in a recent study, found that the economy will need approximately four million additional skilled workers over the next 10 years, thus increasing their numbers by about one-fourth. It is estimated that for every new scientist or engineer that enters the labor force, six or more craftsmen will be needed. The nation's needs for highly educated professional and technical workers will expand at an even greater rate. In 1965, this group comprised almost one-seventh of all jobholders, about one and one-half the proportion of just 10 years earlier. Between now and 1975, the nation's professional manpower requirements will continue to grow at about twice the rate of other labor needs, thus continuing to increase this ratio.

Such an upgrading of the labor force is certainly a desirable, and in most respects inevitable, consequence of a highly developed economy. But if our educational and industrial institutions do not remain alert and responsive to these future needs, the result could be serious dislocations of America's human resources. Even today, some three million jobs remain unfilled because qualified people cannot be found. This situation exists though there are currently more than three million Americans unemployed and seeking work. The possibility of our dynamic economy increasing this disparity between the types of skills needed and those available is great, unless all of us—educators, businessmen, and public administrators—attempt to foresee future changes and adjust our policies accordingly.

Our first effort toward preventing a larger imbalance in the labor markets could be an uplifting of the education of our most deficient workers. About one-half of the nation's total employed have less than a high school education, and almost one-fifth never completed the eighth grade. It is evident that many of these men and women have less than a minimum effective education today and will be even more disadvantaged in the future. If they are not to become tomorrow's unemployables and poverty cases, efforts must be made to improve their education and training and thus improve their usefulness to society.

As should be evident, the challenges that will be faced by education in the future are not exclusive to this one institution; they are truly challenges facing all segments of society. If our educational system is successful in developing the methods and techniques that will be required by the enormous intellectual demands of the future, business has the responsibility of helping to decide what changes can be made, how much they will cost, and how they will be financed. Business can be of particular service by helping educators develop the same scientific decision-making techniques to their problems that have been applied to business decisions and planning for many years. Through this process, the purpose and objectives of our educational system could be more clearly developed. At the same time, more efficient and effective means of achieving these goals could be initiated.

If the challenges of the future are to be met, business and education must in fact greatly increase their interaction. Corporate giving doesn't complete business' responsibility to the world of study and schooling. According to former United States Commissioner of Education Francis Keppel, now president of the General Learning Corporation, "The private sector is knowledgeable and well staffed. It can contribute to the strengthening of both public affairs and private profit by taking an active part in the development of new ways of teaching and learning."

The role of business in education will become increasingly more important in the future. We are entering an age when more than ever before education will become a continuous, life-long process. If we are to keep up with the complex demands of our society, individuals at all age levels will spend an increasing proportion of their time in expanding and extending their education. We have already arrived at a place where our formal education is but the beginning of a long and rewarding learning process. And business, through its own training and eductional programs, can and should foster this process.

We in the United States are presently on the threshold of unlimited and even unimagined progress and change. We have only begun to realize the benefits of our science and technology. Our journey into the Affluent Society has only recently gotten underway. The advantages of our knowledge explosion are not yet even fully conceived. And the success of our efforts to improve the overall quality and culture of our lives is as yet barely perceivable.

But if the nation is to attain its full promise, there are numerous challenges that must be met. Foremost among these are the changes and innovations facing our educational system. Education will need to adapt its techniques and methods to the future demands of our society. It will also need to assure that the substance and purpose of its teaching is appropriate to the needs of our society. Indeed, the responsiveness and imagination of the nation's educators will in the future as in the past largely determine the limits of our success. We must all —businessmen included—see that the appropriate changes are made and that the challenges of the future are not allowed to become the barriers to progress.

The problems and rewards of the future will be truly infinite. We are living in an exciting and demanding age. I'm sure that each of you will accept your responsibility and see that the future's promise and potential are fully realized.

Attempts to pin the responsibility for inflation on the business community and corporate profits cannot be supported by economic facts. If inflation is to be prevented, the government must demonstrate the same resolve and self-discipline that have been asked of the private economy.

5

Prices, Profits, and Politics

Speech before the American Bankers Association, San Francisco, California, October 26, 1966.

As a businessman, I fully appreciate the importance of our highly developed financial system. And the most vital link in this system is the banking industry. Our banks have played an indispensable role in our nation's economic growth and progress. The nation's economy can certainly be only as great as the banking system which supports it.

One year ago the economic outlook was one of reserved confidence and optimism. Though the possible implications of Vietnam had become recognized, it was generally believed the economy could adjust to the new pressures with little difficulty. For five years the nation had enjoyed uninterrupted expansion. And with the appropriate mix of monetary and fiscal policy, it was not unreasonable to expect our resilient economy to move forward for another year.

During the past year these expectations have generally been realized, if not in fact exceeded. But at the same time, other developments have occurred which are causing some anxiety about the future course of business. Stock prices, for example, have declined some 20 percent from their highs of early this year. Interest rates, as you no doubt are reminded of daily, have risen to 40-year highs. And inflation is now more intense than at any time in the past decade. Since the beginning of this year, for example, consumer prices have increased about 3.5 percent, placing inflation in the forefront of public concern.

In addition, such problems as our balance-of-payments deficit, the continued economic troubles in the United Kingdom, and the uncertainties of Vietnam remain serious obstacles to future planning. Thus, it is understandable that questions are being raised by an increasing number of people as to the current outlook. Indeed, with many observers predicting a recession next year, concern over the future state of business is to be expected.

The current level of disquiet is sufficiently disturbing to even the more optimistic among us to make a closer examination of economic conditions timely. If I may then, I would like to offer some views on how the current situation developed and how some of our troubles may be resolved in the future.

As you know, the course of economic activity in the 1960s has been greatly influenced by what has come to be called the "New Economics." Though most of the principles for the New Economics date back to the mid-1930s, these principles had never been as persistently applied as in recent years. The heart of the New Economics is the government's active use of monetary and fiscal tools, especially the latter, to influence business activity. Accordingly, if the economy is slack— unusually high unemployment and a large number of idle plants—the government is to tax less and spend more, thus stimulating economic activity through a budget deficit. Conversely, if the economy becomes overemployed and inflationary, the government is to tax more and spend less, hence slowing down the economy with a budget surplus. Though the simplicity of this description is deceiving, the sophisticated application of these general rules will promote economic growth, full employment, and noninflationary prices.

During the early 1960s when the New Economics was first

actively applied, the seriously underemployed state of the economy called for an expansionary government policy. The success of this expansionary policy in promoting economic growth is now widely recognized. At the end of 1965, the economy was enjoying its longest peacetime expansion in history. Since 1961, output of goods and services had increased by one-third and industrial production had advanced by one-half. In five years, unemployment had been trimmed by nearly two million persons, and the country's idle productive capacity had been eliminated. And all this had been achieved without sacrificing general price stability.

The record of government economic policy over the past year, however, has not been so bright and shining. Nor in some respects could it be labeled a success. Strong economic growth has been sustained for a sixth year, but the gain has been blemished by rising prices. Of even greater long-term consequence, the orderly and balanced conditions of just one year ago no longer exist. The economy today instead is burdened with imbalances and distortions which pose a substantial barrier to future stable growth.

With full benefit of hindsight, we can probably point to July 28, 1965 as the turning point in our recent economic history. On that date, the President announced an increase in our military commitment to Vietnam and thus gave the economic climate a new look. With the addition of a military buildup on an already active economy, the old problem of economic slack was soon removed. In its place a new problem of preventing a fully employed economy from overheating was created.

By early this year, the pressures of the military buildup were becoming evident. Between the President's July announcement and his economic reports in January, unemployment dropped from 4.5 percent to the long-sought goal of 4.0 percent. Industrial utilization rates increased to above 91 percent, with many factories operating well above their desired levels. The added demand of the war buildup was threatening to destroy the economy's stable noninflationary prosperity. The possibility of a condition of excess demand when prices and wages would move up rapidly was becoming increasingly apparent. In only a few months' time the economic situation had changed from one needing stimulation to one requiring restraint.

Through the first eight months of 1966, however, our policymakers did not make the appropriate adjustments to meet the challenge of this new situation. Although the economy was near or above practical full employment, and though prices were increasing at annual rates of 3 to 4 percent, the administration elected not to initiate a policy of general restraint. The rules of the New Economics called for either a reduction in government nondefense spending or possibly even a tax increase, but the administration failed to follow either course of action.

In fact, the impact of government operations during the past year has been only slightly less stimulative than in the early sixties when the economy was severely underutilized and the nation's policies were intentionally expansionary. In fiscal 1966, the federal government's cash budget ran a deficit in excess of $3 billion. Only twice during the past 15 months have the government's receipts matched or exceeded its spending. Such deficits would not seem to be in keeping with either the rules of the New Economics or the inflationary condition of the economy. If there was ever a year in which our budget should have shown a substantial surplus, it would seem to have been this past year.

This does not necessarily suggest that the New Economics was inappropriate when the economy reached a fully employed condition. Its basic principles were probably as suitable for slowing the economy as they had previously been for stimulating it. The real question was not the validity of these principles, but instead, the human element involved in applying them. And from the vantage point of the present, application of these rules became impossible when political expediency parted company with economic necessity.

According to the administration, there were reasons for not implementing a more restrictive policy. There were the uncertainties of Vietnam, the easing in auto sales, and the possibility of "overkill." Another reason not mentioned—but one undoubtedly given considerable weight—was the political difficulties of imposing economic restraint in an election year.

When economic and political objectives agreed, as they did in the early sixties, the New Economics worked smoothly. But when the prescription of less spending or higher taxes seemed politically distasteful, as they did this past year, fiscal policy became virtually inoperative.

I should pause at this point to confirm your suspicions. Twenty-twenty hindsight is no substitute for perfect foresight. And as we all know, there is no certainty in economics. Yet, despite the uncertainties and the absence of perfect knowledge, the administration did not lack for advice to restrain the economy's inflationary pace. Throughout most of the past year, a large number, and probably the majority, of academic economists, businessmen, and bankers urged the administration to apply its own prudence campaign to government spending. Since domestic appropriations have exceeded even the President's requests, this advice does not seem to have had much of an impact.

But the government's inappropriate fiscal policy is only part of this past year's economic story. As the administration was not willing to cool off the economy, it became necessary to shift the burden for preventing inflation—and if possible the responsibility for causing it—to other sectors. This seems to have been done by two methods. First, the Federal Reserve System was heavily relied upon to slow the growth in total spending. And second, selective tools, such as the new and expanded use of guideposts, were used to dissuade wage and price increases as well as expenditures in the private economy.

In contrast to the government's indecisive stand on spending and tax policy, the Federal Reserve System has implemented, perhaps belatedly, a progressively more restrictive policy over most of the past year. Beginning with the discount rate increase in December of 1965, the monetary authorities have responded in full measure to the economy's inflationary pressures. As a result, most interest rates have increased to the highest levels since the 1920s. This has been accompanied by the most aggressive, and in many ways most severe, competition for funds in several decades. And in turn, loans for some purposes—notably home construction—seem to be almost nonexistent.

This sharp escalation of interest rates has caused some distortions and maladjustments in the economy. In addition, the financial markets and banking system have been placed under unusually strong pressures and strains, some of which could cause serious problems in the future. But what is more important is that many of these maladjustments and strains could have been prevented. If the government's spending authorities had supported the banking system's anti-inflationary program with more restrictive measures of its own, some of the current imbalances most likely would not have developed.

Yet, somewhat ironically, when the tight money situation became a political liability, some legislators asserted that the high interest rates resulted from reckless actions by the banking system. There was no mention that most of these conditions resulted from the economy's general inflationary pressures. Nor was there any mention that interest rates need not have gone so high had government spending been less. Instead, legislation was passed urging the bank authorities to impose unrealistic ceilings on some interest rates, a step which might very well create even more financial maladjustments.

The administration also shifted some of its responsibility for preventing inflation—and more recently much of the blame for causing it—to the business community. Earlier this year, under the program of the voluntary wage–price guideposts, the government attempted to roll back a number of price increases. Though some of these efforts met with qualified success, at least from the government's viewpoint, it was soon apparent that the inflationary pressures were too widespread to be held back on a selective basis. In addition, the increasing militancy of labor was proving the guideposts almost completely ineffectual in holding back inflationary wage increases.

Thus the government has developed, at least temporarily, a

more general means of attacking inflation and of shifting the focus away from its own policies to those of the private sector. This has generally been accomplished by suggesting that one of the major causes of the inflation has been the recent increase in business profits. Gardner Ackley, for example, early last spring and again in two recent speeches, implied that profits are excessive and should be reduced. During the summer, a congressman introduced legislation to impose an "excess" profits tax on corporate incomes "to trim the fat from those areas of the economy which are gorging themselves on inflation." Even more pointed have been the comments by the nation's labor leaders. The director of the AFL–CIO's research department stated recently that, "If there is any inflation in the United States today, it is profit inflation . . . they have gone up way out of line with anything else in the economy."

Though these accusations—like those against high interest rates—are satisfying to the uninformed, they shed little light on the nation's economic troubles. In fact they reflect a lack of understanding of the long-term record of profits and of their role in our free market economy.

This is not to deny that profits have posted substantial gains over the current expansion. But there is no basis for asserting that this increase or the current level is excessive. Moreover, viewing the record of only the past five years, which the critics are prone to do, fails to reveal the sensitivity of profits to ups and downs in the business cycle. By using a recession year as the base period, such comparisons result in distortions which are grossly misleading. If profits are viewed over a longer period, a substantially different picture unfolds. For the postwar period, corporate income has grown at a slower rate than

other types of income. From 1950 to 1965, wages and salaries
received by the nation's workers increased almost 150 percent.
In the same 15 years the total spendable earnings of the nation's population advanced 135 percent. By comparison, corporate profits rose only about 95 percent, or substantially less
than the other incomes. Thus, when downturns in business
are included with upturns, corporate profits over the long run
have not posted unusual gains.

Other comparisons of profits from peak to peak offer
equally convincing evidence that profits do not represent an
excessive share of national income. Though the portion of national income going to profits has increased from less than 6
percent in 1960 to about 8 percent late last year, this share is
still below the portion received in 1955 and in 1950. Even the
after-tax return on net worth was lower in 1965 than other
peak years—11.1 percent last year compared with almost 12
percent in 1955 and more than 13 percent in 1950.

These comparisons should suggest that profits are not excessive or out of line with the income going to other segments of
the economy. However, the level of profits need not be justified solely on the basis of their relative growth or their share
of total income. Those who find fault with the current level of
profits—like those who find fault with high interest rates—do
not fully understand the workings of our free market economy. Historically, periods of high profits have also been periods of high wages and high employment.

It does not in fact seem unreasonable to suggest that favorable profit levels are a primary causal force in sustaining economic growth. Much of the strength and longevity of the current expansion, for example, can be attributed to the substan-

tial investment commitments of the business community. Since the beginning of the recovery in 1961, business has increased its annual expenditures on new plants and equipment from $34 billion to $61 billion. These expenditures have helped modernize productive facilities and improve America's competitive position in international markets. In addition, this tremendous increase in investment has helped meet the nation's objective of providing employment for the unemployed and jobs for the new entrants to the labor force.

Business needs to maintain high levels of capital expenditures in the future. With the postwar babies now coming of working age, the labor force is expected to increase by about 15 million persons over the next decade, almost twice the increase in the past 10 years. If these young people are to find jobs, business investment must grow at high rates. In 1965, each production job represented a capital investment of about $25,000—one-third again as large as that invested just five years ago. Such investment commitments will only be forthcoming if profit levels remain sufficiently high to encourage industrial expansion and modernization.

Having spent much of my time developing what went wrong this year, I would now like to offer some thoughts on what lessons the past year holds for future planning. The administration's reluctance to restrain the economy this past year has not, I am sure, resulted from a disinterest in preventing inflation. The President has repeatedly said that restoration of price stability is one of the primary goals of his administration. I am convinced that these statements are offered with genuine sincerity. But I am equally convinced that if inflation is to be prevented, the government must demonstrate the same resolve and self-discipline that have been asked of the private economy. If, because of Vietnam and other forces, a balance is not soon restored between the nation's demand for goods and its capacity to produce, the government must be willing to reduce its domestic spending and possibly even increase taxes until the inflationary pressures ease.

In the short run, as during the past year, such acts of self-discipline may not seem politically agreeable. But I cannot help believing that for the long pull a wise economic policy is also a wise political policy. The nation's elderly and poor, who have seen their purchasing power gradually diminish this year, surely cannot enthusiastically support those political leaders who fail to act decisively in preventing inflation. The same holds true, I believe, for the nation's housewives who are currently up in arms over rising food prices and young families who are trying to buy homes. Should this year's inflation be paid for with a recession next year, the decision not to implement a policy of sufficient prudence earlier this year could become a costly political mistake indeed.

Finally, if the New Economics, despite its earlier success, is not to be remembered as an impractical and unworkable concept, government policymakers must recognize that the nation demands as much economic responsibility under today's inflationary conditions as during the earlier period of unemployment. Decisionmakers must realize that rapidly rising prices are of great concern to the American people. Attempts to blame bankers and businessmen for the current conditions will not be accepted by the public as a substitute for fiscal prudence on the part of government. In the final analysis, primary responsibility for a sound economic climate within which the country can prosper and grow remains squarely with the federal government. We should all insist that this responsibility be more fully demonstrated in the critical period ahead than it has been in the recent past.

*Businessmen should help bring federal
antitrust policies back to their original
goal of promoting effective competition.
Unless these policies are redirected toward
maintaining conditions under which
every business can compete effectively,
they could hamper America's economic
growth.*

6

Antitrust Today:
A Curb on Competition?

Are our antitrust laws, as presently interpreted and enforced, promoting competition, or are they undermining the very thing they were designed to protect?

The antitrust problem is, without a doubt, one of the most complex and difficult now facing the American businessman. The goals of our antitrust policies are easy to define, but it is a different matter when we get down to details and attempt to spell out just how the law should be applied in specific cases.

Historically, our antitrust policies were designed to preserve a highly competitive market system. Through the forces of competition, the nation is assured maximum economic efficiency and economic progress. To assure healthy competition, the antitrust laws were enacted to bar predatory, collusive, and other monopolistic practices. Since these objectives are as desirable today as they were in 1890, when the Sherman Act was passed, maintenance of reasonable and effective antitrust policies is something that every enlightened businessman should and does support.

Because of the complexity of the situation, it would certainly be overly ambitious of me—a layman—to attempt to resolve the nation's many antitrust problems. In fact, I would be hard put just to list in a few minutes the wide range of issues included under the broad heading of antitrust policies. I shall confine myself to only one aspect of these policies. Specifically, I would like to concentrate on recent antitrust developments regarding mergers and acquisitions.

At some time almost every business, large or small, considers combining with another firm or selling its operations. Large firms often want to merge with another company to expand markets, to ensure a source of supply, or possibly to diversify operations. Small and medium-size firms consider mergers for these same reasons. They may also look upon a merger as a means of growth or improving their competitive position against larger firms. In addition, smaller family-owned firms sometimes wish to sell their operations to other companies, frequently for personal reasons—such as the owner's desire to retire or to create an estate for his heirs.

In recent years, however, several disturbing developments have resulted from the government's policies toward mergers and acquisitions. Two of these developments seem especially significant.

First, the Supreme Court has adopted a very narrow interpretation of our antitrust statutes. Consequently, a merger policy is being established which places more emphasis on preserving fragmented markets and a given number of competitors than on promoting competition. By so doing, the purpose and intent of our antitrust legislation is being misdirected. This raises the possibility of detrimental long-run consequences to our nation's economic growth and efficiency.

A second point of concern is that far too many of the government's current policies concerning mergers are being determined by administrative agencies rather than through the more traditional processes of legislation and judicial interpretation. Because of the cost and delay of a court defense, many mergers and acquisitions are halted by the threat of a suit by the Federal Trade Commission or the Antitrust Division. It is possible that many mergers so prevented may in fact have been both legal and desirable.

Economic progress demands dynamic change, and our antitrust laws should not inhibit this change. The freedom to compete and to succeed does not carry with it an assurance of economic immortality. Nor does it carry the obligation for every successful business to continue operating to eternity. A competitive system is characterized by continual change as new firms are born and older ones cease doing business.

The promotion of competition, in other words, is not the same as maintaining a given number of competitors. Instead, competition is a situation under which each businessman realizes that while good judgment and hard work may produce success, a mistake or miscalculation could have severe or fatal consequences. The primary goal of our antitrust policies should be to maintain conditions under which all companies realize that success or failure depends on their ability to compete vigorously and effectively.

Some of the recent merger decisions imply, however, that efficient and aggressive competition may in fact be held suspect. In 1962, for example, in the Brown Shoe Case, the Supreme Court ruled that the Brown Shoe Company could not buy a chain of retail shoe stores even though the acquisition may have been beneficial to consumers. The Court attempted to reconcile its position in this way:

> . . . some of the results of large integrated or chain operations are beneficial to consumers. Their expansion is not rendered unlawful by the mere fact that small independent stores may be adversely affected. It is competition, not competitors, which the

Act protects. But we cannot fail to recognize Congress' desire to promote competition through the protection of viable, small, locally-owned businesses. Congress appreciated that higher costs and prices might result from maintenance of fragmented industries and markets. It resolved these competing considerations in favor of decentralization.

The contradiction in this ruling—competition is good so long as no one gets hurt—has given many people cause for concern. Donald Turner, for example, now head of the Justice Department's Antitrust Division, had this to say before leaving his post at Harvard Law School:

> I find no credible support for the statement in Brown Shoe that Congress consciously appreciated the possible efficiency cost of attempting to preserve fragmented industries and consciously resolved the competing considerations in favor of decentralization.

In the same article, Dr. Turner also took issue with the Foremost Dairies Case decision where the Federal Trade Commission held a merger illegal because Foremost's ". . . overall organization gives it a decisive advantage in efficiency over its smaller rivals." Dr. Turner commented that "this position is not only bad economics but bad law."

However, Dr. Turner's interest in placing primary emphasis on maintaining competition rather than on protecting competitors has not been fully shared by the Supreme Court. As recently as May of this year, in the Von's Grocery Company Case, the Court ruled that the merger of two small grocery store chains was illegal, though their combined sales were only 7.5 percent of the large Los Angeles market. Here again the Court supported the thesis of "the more competitors the better." It placed unusual emphasis upon the decline in single-store firms from 5,365 in 1950, to 3,818 in 1961. The majority interpreted this decline as decisive evidence that the Los Angeles grocery retail market showed a trend toward monopoly, a trend which would be accelerated if the Von's merger was allowed to stand.

To interpret a decline in single-store grocery firms as a lessening of competition seems questionable. Such an interpretation must presume that there exists a direct relationship between the number of stores and the level of competition, with more firms indicating more competition. Those of us in business realize that this is not necessarily true. All firms do not contribute equally to competition. Oftentimes the merger of two small firms increases their efficiency and enhances their ability to compete effectively in a given market.

In his dissent to the Von's decision, Justice Stewart disputed the majority's findings and concluded that a more careful analysis of the evidence suggested that competition in the retail food market in Los Angeles was very lively. In support of his conclusion, he noted that the market share of the leading grocery chain in Los Angeles, as well as the combined share of the largest two, three, four, and five firms, had declined in recent years. And even though the combined shares of the top 20 firms in the market increased slightly beween 1948 and 1958, seven of the top firms in 1958 were not even in existence as chains in 1948.

Justice Stewart also pointed out that much of the decline in single-store firms probably resulted from these firms forming chains in order to compete more effectively in this large market. And, finally, he said that more weight should have been given to the market extension characteristics of the merger in question and to a District Court finding that in the four years since the merger no evidence could be found that competition had been lessened.

Justice Stewart's dissent in this significant case reveals the inadequacies of the Court's increasing reliance on mathematical ratios. Because of the diversity of our various markets and the complexity of our economy, a single concentration ratio does not accurately reflect the level of competition.

But the importance of the Von's case is found not so much in the majority's rationale as in the implications this decision holds for future mergers and acquisitions. The Von's decision could have significant impact on the expansion and diversification plans of all businesses, small and large alike.

In the Von's case, the Court prevented two successful, local, largely family-owned concerns from combining their retail outlets. The fact that each had less than 5 percent of the Los Angeles market and neither had any previous history of mergers or acquisitions would seem to refute the assumption that these two firms were attempting to monopolize the market. Instead, the evidence suggests that by merging they hoped to extend their market coverage and compete more effectively throughout the large Los Angeles area. In a sense, as Justice Stewart noted, by preventing this merger, "the defendants are being punished for the sin of aggressive competition."

Should this decision continue as a firm precedent for future court and administrative actions, a great many future mergers could be challenged. In fact, this decision could go far toward eliminating the merger or acquisition route to the small successful businessman who wishes to sell his business. Business skill is a scarce resource in our society, and it should be encouraged in every way. One such encouragement is the entrepreneur's knowledge that at any given time he can, if he wishes, easily find a good market for his business. If the market is severely restricted, as the Von's decision seems to do, this could have a depressing effect on the birth of new firms.

The Von's decision also seems to discourage attempts by business to achieve increased efficiencies through mergers. The adverse impact on the economy of preventing mergers which are likely to result in cost savings could be severe. Donald Turner, before assuming his responsibilities at the Antitrust Division, gave the following persuasive reasons for not enforcing such a restrictive merger policy:

> To forbid mergers that would or might produce substantial efficiencies would narrow substantially the category of acceptable mergers, thereby drastically weakening the market for capital assets and seriously depreciating the price that entrepreneurs could get for their businesses when they wish to liquidate. Such a policy would seriously interfere with maximum exploitation of productive resources; and not only might it have adverse long-run effects on entry and growth of small businesses, but it would also be clearly against the interests of small businesses already in being. . . .

Despite these compelling arguments, the Von's case and other recent decisions suggest that the current trend is toward a more restrictive policy. This trend is particularly evident in the Court's recent use of the concept of so-called "potential competition." In the El Paso–Pacific Northwest case, for example, an acquisition was stopped on the grounds that even though at the time Pacific Northwest did not operate in El Paso's market, at some future date the two companies might become competitors in the same market if they were not allowed to merge. Thus, the Court has added to its antimerger weapons by assuming the ability to predict future business behavior.

The Supreme Court's narrow interpretation of antitrust law is only one part of the current merger policy problem facing business. Because of the general language of the antitrust laws and limitations to expedient and economical litigation, an increasingly large amount of merger policy is being determined at the administrative level of government. Should this trend continue, businessmen could eventually see most merger cases removed from the checks and balances of the judicial system.

The Federal Trade Commission and the Antitrust Division of the Justice Department were each established to enforce our antitrust laws. It was their purpose to analyze various business practices and initiate antitrust action where needed. This is surely a necessary function which must be performed if our laws are to be effective.

However, as a result of the Supreme Court's reliance on such concepts as mathematical ratios and the increasing cost of litigating antitrust suits, these agencies have in recent years developed enormous power. Moreover, the presumption of guilt shifts the burden of proof from the Justice Department to the defendant. Since many firms are not able or willing to defend an antitrust suit through the courts, a threat of action by either agency often forces a company to drop a merger proposal.

Just this past month, for example, two small banks in Pennsylvania dropped merger plans after the Justice Department attacked the proposal. As the plans had previously been analyzed and approved by the Comptroller of the Currency, it is possible that the Justice Department's actions were not warranted. But as the banks were not financially able to defend their proposal in court, the threat of an antitrust suit was sufficient to terminate their plans.

Given the scope and language of the Von's decision, the activities of the Antitrust Division and the Federal Trade Commission may be expanded even more in the future. Such an expansion would probably go even further toward removing antitrust policy formulation from the judicial and legislative branches and giving it to the administrative branch. Ceding the regulatory agencies even greater authority over mergers and acquisitions will most likely only increase the uncertainties and inconsistencies which already exist in the antitrust area.

I shall summarize my major points and offer some thoughts *Summary* as to how the nation's antitrust policy can be improved. Our antitrust laws were formulated to prevent monopolies and to maintain competition. Through the interplay of competitive markets, the consumer is protected from the abuses of monopolistic practices and society is assured maximum benefit of all resources. These are certainly objectives which we all support.

However, recent interpretations of the antitrust laws seem to have replaced the objective of maintaining competition with the questionable goal of protecting competitors. The courts are increasingly relying on mathematical ratios and other arbitrary measures as indicators of competition and ignoring empirical evidence concerning the competitive impact of a given merger. As a result, decisions have been handed down that are not always in the best interest of the public or of our competitive system. In fact, in their efforts to maintain fragmented markets, the courts and regulatory agencies have probably often reduced effective competition.

If the nation is to maintain competitive markets, our antitrust policy must be redirected. And if our nation's antitrust policy is to be redirected, the business community must assume much of the initiative.

Business, for example, should not hesitate to point out through speeches, letters to congressmen and other means, the possible consequences of recent government efforts to maintain markets that are inconsistent with our technological and industrial achievements. In keeping with our belief in the competitive system, we must emphasize how current antitrust policy works at cross purposes with the nation's economic objectives of maximum growth and development. Unless the political and social environment surrounding antitrust policy becomes more enlightened, business cannot expect necessary improvements in antitrust policy.

Business must also be more vocal in explaining its reasons for proposing mergers and acquisitions. Each proposal should be analyzed from an economic as well as a legal viewpoint, and the public should be informed of the benefits that are possible. If efficiencies or economies are expected, these should be highlighted in public announcements.

In addition, painful though it may be, business must be more willing to resist antitrust suits in the courts. By challenging the government's interpretations and economic theories, we can attempt to establish a more viable antitrust policy. Further, if the business community challenges more of these suits and achieves some success, the Federal Trade Commission and the Antitrust Division will scrutinize more carefully those mergers which they challenge. Hopefully, this will result in a more reasonable and consistent interpretation of antitrust laws.

Finally, businessmen should encourage and support an in-depth study of the nation's merger policy and the potential impact of this policy on competition and our other economic objectives. Such a study should be directed to recent merger cases or proposals that have been either successfully or unsuccessfully challenged by the government. In view of the number of recent cases, sufficient evidence should be available to determine if, in retrospect, the government's actions against these mergers were desirable on the basis of subsequent economic developments. In particular, the study could use empirical data of competitive conditions before and after such merger proposals, and decide if the proposal did in fact threaten to "substantially lessen competition."

I would not presume to try to outline each area which such a study might cover. But I believe that at least three questions must be considered:

First, does our current antitrust policy sufficiently direct itself to the objective of maintaining competitive markets? Second, is the level of competition in a market accurately reflected by the number of competitors or some given concentration ratio? And, third, because of the difficulties of predicting future business behavior in a given market, are the government's and courts' current efforts to forecast "potential competition" defensible?

Based on the findings of this study, it should be possible to propose new legislation to improve our antitrust policy. If, as a result of such a study new laws are considered, business must be willing to testify at hearings and to make suggestions in the public forum.

As participants in a free market economy and supporters of vigorous competition, each businessman has a responsibility to help redirect the nation's antitrust policy. To this responsibility, I commend your attention and effort.

The U.S. should place less reliance on temporary expedients and instead adopt long-range programs to improve the nation's competitive position in world markets. A fundamental condition for expanding our exports is a restoration of price aand wage stability to the American economy.

7

The Balance of Payments: The Need for a New Approach

Speech before the Miami–Dade County Chamber of Commerce, Miami, Florida, January 16, 1967.

In recent years, both at home and abroad, an issue of continuing concern among public officials, economists, and businessmen has been the U.S. balance of payments. Various individuals and groups have explored in great detail the implications of the persistent deficit in our international accounts. There has been a variety of proposals on how the disparity between America's international payments and receipts can be eliminated. And seldom does our own government implement major domestic programs without first considering the impact on America's international economic position.

In simple terms, our country's balance of payments is a record of economic transactions on the part of government, business, and individuals with their counterparts in the rest of the world. It is a summary statement of America's total payments to other countries and total receipts from these countries. Included in these payments and receipts are such items as imports and exports, direct foreign investments, interest and dividends, international loans, and military and foreign aid. The balance of payments, in other words, reveals how the United States pays its way internationally.

A deficit in a nation's balance of payments occurs when, except for the so-called balancing items, its receipts from abroad are not sufficient to cover its payments abroad. Moreover, as a deficit suggests a country is spending more than it is earning, the deficit is frequently regarded, though sometimes mistakenly, as a danger signal. Some observers believe that when a nation has a deficit in its international accounts it is living beyond its means and will eventually deplete its international reserves. This, too, can be a mistaken belief.

With but one exception, the United States has sustained a deficit in its international payments every year since 1950. During the early part of this period, the excess of U.S. payments over receipts was not considered a serious problem, if in fact a problem at all. The political and economic strength of the United States after World War II led it to become the leading international banker, foreign aid provider, military protector and producer of the Free World. We believed that our own security would be enhanced by using our public and private capital to facilitate the recovery of Western Europe and other nations around the world. Our efforts proved so successful that the international community welcomed our deficit and the resulting outflow of dollars. Moreover, because of their confidence in the dollar, most nations preferred dollar claims in their reserve accounts to non-interest-bearing gold.

Beginning in the late 1950s, however, the magnitude of our payments deficit, and the international attitude concerning it, changed. In 1958, the imbalance between our foreign receipts and our expenditures jumped to over $3 billion, almost three times the average level through the early 1950s. It remained at relatively high levels through 1964. Not until the past two years did the deficit again drop to the $1 billion range.

Even with this recent reduction of the deficit, the U.S. has not been able to remove all the anxieties of the international economic community. Because of the persistence and size of our deficits, some monetary authorities abroad have cast doubt on the ability of the United States to keep the dollar strong and to maintain its world-wide commitments without accepting drastic internal and external policy changes.

If our payments situation is placed in proper perspective, much of the alarm currently being generated is not justified. When an individual's spending exceeds his income, we do not necessarily conclude that he is headed for bankruptcy. Before forming an opinion, we usually examine his financial situation more closely and attempt to determine why the shortage occurred. If he has a strong asset position and has borrowed in order to undertake investments which may later increase his income, we are likely to conclude that he is financially sound. It is his overall situation as to assets and liabilities that concerns us, not the fact that his income and outflow are unequal.

The same consideration should apply to a country's international accounts. In our own case, such an analysis would reveal that the present deficit does not reflect a basic weakness in our overall financial position. On the contrary, America's economic strength remains unequalled by any other nation in the world. The U.S. economy is, in fact, so large and growing so rapidly that the *annual increase* in our national output of goods and services far exceeds the *total annual output* of most other countries in the world.

This strength is readily apparent, even if we limit our attention to our international economic activity. Our commodity exports, for example, have exceeded our commodity imports in every year since the beginning of this century. In the past five years alone, our net merchandise surplus has averaged about $5 billion per year, hardly a sign of a weak economy. Moreover, at the end of 1965, U.S. assets and investments abroad were valued at above $100 billion, about twice the total foreign assets and investments in the United States. The fundamental economic situation of the United States is one of strength.

Our deficit does not reflect a basic weakness in the dollar or in our economy. Instead, it reflects our long-term military, foreign aid, and investment commitments to the Free World, as well as our role as international banker. There are, however, reasons for seeking a balance in our international payments. As a result of our long-standing deficit, at the end of last year we owed about $27 billion to foreign individuals and institutions. Approximately one-half of this total was held by foreign central banks, thus making it immediately eligible for exchange into our gold should these authorities so desire.

Along with the growth of these short-term liabilities, our official gold holdings have been declining. At the end of 1957, our gold reserves amounted to $23 billion. They are now down to about half this amount. It is clear that if we continue to lose gold at this rate, our gold supply will be exhausted. Thus, even though the United States is the world's largest producer, trader, and consumer of goods and services, continued depletion of our gold reserves could undermine the confidence in the convertibility of the dollar into gold and thereby disrupt the international monetary system.

Recognizing this potential danger, the last three administrations have assigned a high priority to reducing our balance-of-payments deficit. But most of the policies put into effect so far have been highly selective and have resulted in undesirable restraints or controls, particularly on the free flow of trade and capital. In 1959, for example, economic aid to developing countries was tied, where possible, to American sources of supply. Two years later, those countries where American military forces were stationed were asked to increase their military purchases from the United States. In 1963 and again in 1965, portfolio investments in foreign-developed countries were discouraged by the interest equalization tax. And most recently, a comprehensive voluntary restraint program was implemented to discourage U.S. loans and direct investments abroad.

Some of these measures have met with limited success, but the long-term wisdom of the current strategy leaves much to be desired. Far too often, these programs tend to weaken rather than enhance our fundamental balance-of-payments position. Many may be costly, stopgap measures—measures that offer only moderate short-term improvement at the risk of damaging our long-term political and economic objectives.

One example is the tying of foreign aid to U.S. goods. At times, these same goods could be obtained elsewhere at a lower price. By requiring the recipients to spend their money inefficiently, we lose their goodwill and reduce the effectiveness of our foreign aid program. This policy also encourages recipient nations to introduce selective controls or import licensing—thus working at cross purposes with our long-term objective of free trade. In addition, the belief that our goods were not competitive in such instances has, rightly or wrongly, tended to attach a stigma to all goods of U.S. origin, including those that are clearly competitive in foreign markets. This may be one important reason why countries that receive our aid often seem to shun purchases of competitively priced U.S. products that are not aid-financed.

A question can also be raised concerning restrictions on the amount of foreign purchases that American tourists can bring back duty-free. These restrictions are reported to have caused considerable bitterness and resentment toward the United States. The hardest hit have been those countries where U.S. tourists provide an important source of livelihood and foreign exchange earnings. This is especially true of Western Hemisphere countries, such as those in Latin America. Here, the United States—being by far the most important trading partner—would actually stand to lose few, if any, of these tourist dollars. Most of the money spent in these countries would soon return in payment for U.S. goods and services. In any event, even if these restrictions on tourist purchases have enhanced our balance of payments, the resulting loss of goodwill toward the United States may have more than offset this gain.

The interest equalization tax on foreign securities and loans also seems to have had adverse effects on the world economy. This program, which was designed to reduce the attractiveness of foreign securities to American investors, has caused some serious side effects. Insofar as this tax has actually reduced the outflow of funds from the United States, it has tended to raise interest rates abroad. At the same time—and partially reflecting the higher interest rates—it has tended to depress the value of foreign equities. Perhaps one of the most vivid examples of the sensitivity of the foreign stock values to the various effects of this tax was the sharp decline in the Japanese stock market that immediately followed the announcement of the tax in 1963. This measure may have reduced our balance-of-payments deficit, but it may have done so at the expense of foreign financial markets.

Perhaps the most questionable payments control has been

the voluntary restraints applied to direct investment outflows. By encouraging companies to borrow abroad, this program has placed unusual pressure on foreign capital markets and has caused resentment against U.S. companies operating abroad. In addition, it has been a highly inefficient means of improving our international payments. It has impaired, for example, the usefulness of our own money and capital markets to Europeans. As a result, it has also weakened the incentive for these countries to maintain their dollar deposits and other financial assets in this country. Moreover, since the restraint program increased interest rates and equity earnings ratios abroad, we have encouraged foreign investors to shift their investments from the U.S. to other nations. Finally, the voluntary restraint program has caused American companies to borrow abroad at high fees and interest costs, thus shifting earnings from these loans out of the U.S. to foreign banks and investors.

This program, in short, could have a serious effect on our long-term payments position. Dollars invested overseas are, after all, a means of generating future income for the United States. Over the past few years, our private investments abroad have made a substantial positive contribution to the balance of payments. In 1965, for example, foreign investments resulted in a favorable contribution to our international payments of about $3 billion. Even this contribution fails to include the additional exports which are indirectly stimulated by the activities of local U.S. plants and marketing organizations abroad. Thus, government actions that jeopardize the competitive position of U.S. business overseas prevent effective management of assets that are of enormous value to the United States. Further, these programs could substantially weaken our long-term payments position.

Taking all these factors into account, our economy, as well as the economies of our friends abroad, is paying a dear price for our moderately reduced balance-of-payments deficit. This does not, however, suggest that the U.S. business community should withdraw its support from the administration's current policy. Recognizing the impact of our commitments in Southeast Asia, American businessmen have responded to the government's request and in some cases even exceeded their guidelines. Total net capital outflows, for example, fell from about $7 billion in 1964 to less than $4 billion a year later. Under the current critical conditions, it is necessary for business to continue to comply with the present national policy.

Because of the inconsistencies stemming from the present controls, however, the business community should insist that improved programs be adopted for the future. Instead of proliferating, intensifying, and perpetuating selective controls, we must develop more positive programs which promise a long-term solution to our balance-of-payments situation.

If we continue to rely on short-term expedients, our resolve in pursuing more fundamental solutions may be weakened. To the extent that our present balance-of-payments programs have increased our government's willingness to tolerate the inflation of the last 18 months, the ultimate cost of these programs has been greatly increased.

It is increasingly evident that the time has come to develop new approaches to this problem. The time has come to adopt programs that are compatible with our national and international goals. We can begin by asking some basic questions. For example:

- Is our program of selective controls leading us and the rest of the world in the direction that is most desirable?
- Over the long run, what kind of international political, economic, and financial arrangements are in the best interest of the United States and the rest of the world?
- Are we managing our nation's affairs in a way most likely to help us achieve our internal and external objectives?

It is evident that any program aimed at solving our payments deficit must recognize the vital importance of American exports. In 1965, if our exports had been just 5 percent greater, the deficit in our balance of payments would have been eliminated. Moreover, such an increase in exports would have had the same immediate effect on our international payments as a 40 percent reduction in our direct investment outflow, a 55 percent reduction in our travel expenditures abroad, or a 110 percent increase in foreign travel expenditures in the U.S. These figures clearly suggest that, if we are to reduce our deficit, we must begin by working together to improve our export performance.

The American business community has an urgent and immediate responsibility in this effort. We must do an even better job of eliminating inefficiencies and reducing costs of production so our goods will be more competitive abroad. All of us, both as individual companies and through our trade associations, must do a better job of promoting and selling U.S. goods in foreign markets. The return on these efforts could be substantial. In addition to increasing the market for our goods and services, success in this program would permit the gradual removal of the undesirable selective controls.

But the most necessary and fundamental condition for expanding U.S. exports—a condition toward which government fiscal and monetary policy must lead the way— is a restoration of price and wage stability to the American economy. Over the past two years, excessive demand and inflationary pressures have had a marked and adverse impact on our trade balance. As our incomes have risen and as prices have edged upward, our competitive position in international markets has steadily deteriorated. As a result, our surplus of commodity exports over commodity imports—once a very bright spot in the balance-of-payments picture—has been trending downward. Compared with a trade surplus of nearly $7 billion in 1964, the surplus declined to about $5 billion in 1965, and fell below $4 billion in the year just completed. If this trend is to be halted, and hopefully reversed, a balanced monetary and fiscal policy must again restore noninflationary conditions to the American economy.

In dealing with our balance-of-payments problem, we have now for several years followed a path of stopgap, selective measures. In the current circumstances, we cannot immediately change paths and start anew. But as businessmen, we can and should discuss quite frankly the shortcomings of our present approach and try to throw light on the fundamental weaknesses of the present programs.

Each of us should evaluate the effects of these programs and offer constructive alternatives. I am confident that through business participation a new and better approach to the problem will be realized.

The important question is not can *we eliminate poverty, but rather* how *the task should be carried out. A lasting solution calls for measures to make the poor self-supporting, rather than public-supported.*

8

The Guaranteed Income:
What Does It Guarantee?

Speech before the 46th Annual Massachusetts Safety Conference, Boston, Massachusetts, March 2, 1967.

The U.S. economy has enjoyed strong and healthy growth over most of the 20th century. Even taking into account the Great Depression, industrial production increased about 15 times in the first two-thirds of this century. During the same period, the nation's total employment tripled, and productivity of the average worker improved by a factor of four. The nation's output of goods and services in constant dollars rose about nine times. And the personal consumption expenditures of the typical American—again in constant dollars—increased more than four times.

The nation's strong economic growth, which accelerated in recent years, has provided the American people with unparalleled affluence. Some 25 percent of American households own at least two cars today, about double the comparable percentage as recently as 1961. In addition, about 1.5 million households own at least three cars. Approximately a quarter of U.S. homes boast two or more TV sets. And color TV, which was virtually nonexistent when the 1960s began, is now found in about one home in seven that has television.

Despite the nation's prosperity—or perhaps more accurately because of it—Americans have in recent years become greatly concerned about the problem of poverty. Even though the nation's general economic welfare is at unprecedented levels, we have been made increasingly aware of the large number of Americans who are not yet full members of the Affluent Society. We are, in fact, continually reminded that even after six years of sustained prosperity, some 30 million Americans are classified as poor, and an additional 15 million live barely above what the government defines as a minimum level of subsistence and decency.

It is not difficult to understand why poverty has become such an acute issue during a period of prosperity. Our very affluence has allowed us to tackle social problems that during an earlier period would have been considered inevitable. To be sure, as the first nation in history to lift the great mass of its population substantially above a level of bare subsistence, we have now become concerned with that small portion of the population which has been left behind. We have, in fact, become dedicated to the task of giving all Americans the opportunity for economic security.

The objective of removing economic privation from the national scene commends itself to all Americans. And our nation's resources and wealth are surely sufficient to make this objective feasible. The important question today, however, is not *can* we eliminate poverty, but rather *how* should the task be carried out. Our resources are ample for the job at hand, but they should not be used unwisely. We must be concerned not only with raising the income of our poor, but also with finding the most efficient and effective means of achieving this aim. We must in fact—as we pursue this commendable goal —be constantly alert to what is in the best long-term interest of our country and our people.

With this as a backdrop, I would like to consider one of the recent proposals for eliminating poverty—the guaranteed annual income. According to this proposal, all Americans who are poor—which is roughly defined by the government as a family receiving less than a $3,000 annual income—would automatically receive a supplement from the government, large enough to raise them out of the low income category. In other words, the government would assure all individuals and families of a specified minimum income—an income of sufficient size to afford them a comfortable living.

The advocates of the guaranteed income describe their approach to eliminating poverty as a logical consequence of forces currently at play in our society. They maintain that economic deprivation results in large part from the elimination of jobs by automation and cybernation. They further see the impact of this trend becoming even more acute in the future. As technological change continues apace, these observers believe an increasingly larger share of our labor force will become unemployable and unable to earn a decent income by working.

Consequently, some of the advocates of the guaranteed income propose that the traditional relationship between income and work must be broken. They say that instead of having people work for a living, we will need to adopt the concept of an absolute constitutional right to an income. This would guarantee every citizen of the United States an income from the federal government sufficient to live with dignity. This right, at least as some observers see it, would be above reproof and could not be suspended or limited for any reason.

Other proponents of an income guarantee, however, are not so willing to separate income and work, or more importantly, to divorce income from incentive. In fact, the most widely accepted version of the guaranteed income is a concept referred to as a negative income tax. According to this idea, a minimum income level would still be assured by the government, but a system of incentives would be worked into the program so that the recipients would be encouraged to supplement the government subsidy by their own labor.

A typical explanation of the negative income tax would call for the government to establish a minimum poverty income of, say, $3,000 a year. The government would then stand ready to provide a subsidy of up to 50 percent of the amount that the family income fell below that figure. If the family had no income, for example, the subsidy would be $1,500. If it had an earned income of $1,500, the subsidy would be $750. If it earned $2,500, the subsidy would be $250.

The simplicity of these antipoverty measures has generated much interest. A growing number of economists, politicians, and others have proposed that some version of the guaranteed income would offer the most effective method of solving the poverty problem. They have also added that the direct nature of this approach—particularly if the guaranteed income was substituted for the large and growing number of diverse welfare programs presently in operation—would afford administrative cost reductions and improve the overall efficiency of the government's welfare role. They have also argued that direct payments to the poor, based solely on an individual's income level—such as those called for under the guaranteed income concept—would enhance the recipient's freedom of choice and action.

The arguments for the guaranteed income have been sufficiently convincing to move some parties to action. Within recent months such groups as the President's Commission on Technology, Automation, and Economic Freedom and the White House Conference "To Fulfill These Rights" have considered the possibility of income guarantees. President Johnson, only two months ago, said that he would appoint a commission of leading Americans to examine the idea of a guaranteed income and make a recommendation to the American people. And the U.S. Chamber of Commerce recently held a symposium to consider the concept and its many implications.

The promoters of the guaranteed income, however, appear to have overlooked or deemphasized some of its more serious drawbacks. We may agree that it is more efficient to administer one government program—such as the guaranteed income—than to operate a multitude of different and in many cases overlapping local, state, and federal welfare programs. But at the same time we should question if the guaranteed income would in fact work as smoothly as its advocates have assumed.

There is, for example, a strong possibility that the guaranteed income would become a *supplement* for the current welfare programs rather than—as has been proposed—a *substitute* for these programs. The various welfare policies currently in effect were developed as a result of society's demands and the political response to these demands. Unless the programs have in the meantime lost their initial voter appeal, it seems unlikely that Congress would suddenly—or even eventually—disband the old system in deference to a new and supposedly more efficient method of meeting the nation's welfare needs. If history is a good guide, it seems more likely that the guaranteed income would be superimposed on the programs already in existence, thus increasing rather than reducing the inefficiencies of the government's welfare function.

The possibility of administrative efficiencies aside, it is also doubtful that the guaranteed income is the most effective way to eliminate poverty. All current welfare programs have been developed to meet a specific and presumably pressing need. Different programs have been developed to deal with our older citizens, our disabled, our veterans, and our dependent children, to name but a few. By contrast, the guaranteed income would not differentiate between its recipients. All members of society below the poverty line would receive an income subsidy from the government. This subsidy might be inadequate for some and excessive for others. But even more important, this indiscriminate procedure would not differentiate between those individuals who were unable to support themselves and thus *in need of* welfare and those who could support themselves but *preferred* welfare to earning their own way. Such a sweeping approach to the nation's welfare needs could prove to be a very costly way of meeting our responsibility to the poor.

The advocates of the guaranteed income may, in fact, have misdirected the major thrust of their efforts. They appear to believe that poverty is exclusively a question of inadequate income. Some have even suggested that all the poor need is more money, and once they receive it the problem will be solved. "The initial step on the way to eliminate poverty," one such spokesman recently said, "is to supply money rather than moral uplift, cultural refinements, extended education, or retraining programs."

Many of those knowledgeable about poverty could not disagree more. Those who work closely with the poor maintain instead that freedom from want is more than freedom from hunger and exposure—it is being allowed the opportunity to earn a decent living, to enjoy economic security, and to recognize one's potential. To be meaningful, freedom from want must, they insist, include hope—hope for a better life and a more fulfilling life.

It is this element of hope that has been overlooked by the social engineers of the guaranteed income. More than 60 percent of America's poor are unskilled and about 80 percent did not complete high school. In most cases their poverty is a natural outgrowth of low education, low skill, and low motivation. Knowing nothing but a seemingly endless cycle of poverty, they have little incentive for expecting a better life, or for that matter, going out and working for it.

"The job of eradicating poverty," Vice President Humphrey has said, "will be a long and difficult one because we cannot simply buy a new way of life for people. It is much more than just a question of money. We must re-educate, re-energize, and re-inspire them. To the extent that such constructive efforts can be supplemented through economic resources, our society can and must make the investment."

In other words, a low income is only the outward sign of poverty; its causes are much more complex and not so readily visible. A lasting solution consists of more than a guaranteed income—or, more specifically, a redistribution of income from those above the poverty level to those below the poverty level. A lasting solution calls instead for measures to make the poor self-supporting, rather than public-supported.

Representative Thomas Curtis recently put it: ". . . we must resist the present-day simplicity and speak of providing for the opportunity to earn an income, not providing the income itself." He is saying that we need to educate the uneducated, train the unskilled, and employ the unemployed. We need to provide the poor with those skills and abilities that are required in today's labor market and then see that the available jobs match the available workers. These are ambitious goals; but they must be achieved if our nation's prosperity is not to be tarnished by a large number of unemployable and poverty-stricken workers.

None of the advocates of the guaranteed annual income has satisfactorily answered one of the most important questions —namely, how the program would affect individual incentives. It does not seem unlikely, though, to assume that if an individual was working at an income approaching or slightly above the guaranteed level, he would soon decide it might be preferable to quit work and live off the public sector. Though most Americans are no doubt dedicated to the principle of earning their own way, there would certainly be an element that would take advantage of the government's generosity. And as the fellow workers of this element viewed the benefits of a work-free life, some of them too might be induced to give up work. Thus, by reducing the incentive to work and support oneself, the guaranteed annual income could gradually increase the nonproductive members of society, rather than decrease their numbers.

The most damaging effect of this erosion of incentive could be on the nation's young people—particularly those who come from poor homes. If they were reared in a family which was supported by the government and which lacked respect for personal initiative and individual achievement, they would probably not be inspired to better their own lot through education, training, and hard work. If their family had been supported by a guaranteed income, the route of least resistance for the young person would in fact be to wait until he too became eligible for a guaranteed livelihood. Such attitudes would perpetuate poverty rather than eliminate it. One can even conceive of a situation where the portion of our population receiving a guaranteed income would increase over time rather than decrease. Eventually, the support of this large and growing body of nonworkers could become a costly and unsupportable burden on our economy.

The potential impact of these crosscurrents on the national economy cannot be underestimated. The most vital force in the war on poverty continues to be a strong and healthy economy. A report last year revealed that with a fixed definition of poverty, the number of poor in the U.S. declined three-fourths of the way toward total elimination between 1929 and 1962. This occurred over a period when the government was not pursuing an active war on poverty. Even during the relatively short span of the current expansion, Professor Otto Eckstein of Harvard University says that the number of persons and families below the poverty line has diminished by seven million, from over 22 percent to less than 17 percent of all Americans.

If economic privation is to be eliminated without sacrificing the nation's other long-term goals, we must continue to encourage stable and strong economic growth. The Western world, and particularly the United States, has gained steadily rising economic efficiency over the past several years. This, in turn, suggests that we have been using our supplies of labor, capital, and natural resources better and better. We have been getting more output from given inputs of these productive resources. If this desirable trend is to continue we must continue to offer every incentive to our people to work and to strive for personal improvement.

It is in this light—giving due respect to the nation's past success and its future goals—that we must study and evaluate the guaranteed income. Groups that have great knowledge of worker psychology and individual behavior can contribute to this task. You can advise us on how a guaranteed income could affect incentives and motivations—how it would affect the relationship between human endeavor and material reward. You can help evaluate the influence of a guaranteed income on attitudes and work habits and thus the performance of our labor force. And when you have assessed these issues, you need to communicate your findings to the public and to Congress. When action is taken on the guaranteed income, we must see that it is based on full knowledge of the possible consequences of this proposal.

But you—and all other businessmen—have an even wider responsibility in this area of social needs. We cannot consider the guaranteed income as an isolated attempt to reduce poverty. Instead we need to evaluate this latest, and perhaps most revolutionary, proposal in a broader context—in the context of our total efforts to provide all Americans a decent living. As we study the implications of the guaranteed income, we must at the same time gauge the efficiency and effectiveness of the government's other welfare programs. We must determine which programs are meeting the nation's objectives and which ones are not. We must, in effect, apply the same analytical tools and sound business principles to the area of social welfare that we apply to our daily business decisions.

The goal of eliminating poverty can and should be realized. But if we are not, in the process, to undermine the strength and vitality of our economic system, we must formulate an orderly and reasoned approach to the problem. We must indeed become fully aware of what the guaranteed income guarantees.

There is a great demand today for more and better public services at the local and state levels. Businessmen can help by acting as consultants to their state and local governments on methods to improve overall efficiency.

9

State and Local Governments in a Changing Society

Speech before the Oklahoma Community Achievement Award Banquet, Oklahoma City, Oklahoma, April 12, 1967.

Over the past several years, one of the fastest growing sectors in our economy has been the state and local governments. In just 10 years these governmental bodies have increased their employment almost 60 percent. Over the same period their payrolls more than doubled, rising to $3.5 billion, and their total expenditures have nearly doubled, increasing to about $80 billion. State and local expenditures have, in fact, grown about twice as fast as federal outlays and presently account for more than three-fourths of all government civilian expenditures.

State and local government operations have indeed become big business—and a growth industry of the first magnitude. What are the forces and trends that have caused these units of government to undertake such an enormous expansion in their operations? Have these governmental bodies developed the appropriate organizational, institutional, and financial framework to perform their functions effectively? Finally, what role can and should the business community play in helping these governments do a better job in meeting their responsibilities?

One of the most obvious forces causing the recent surge in state and local government activities has been the rapid growth in population and the attending shift of this population to the metropolitan areas. Since the end of World War II, the nation's total population has increased by about one-third, receiving a particularly strong boost from the postwar baby boom. The population of the nation's metropolitan areas grew

105

at an even faster rate, rising one and one-half times as fast as the total population. As a result, fully 70 percent of all Americans are concentrated in urban areas today.

Another factor that has contributed to the growth in state and local government expenditures has been the nation's growing commitment to education. Not only have we had more people to educate, but we have also attempted to give each person a better education. School and college enrollment for the present year is up almost 50 percent from just 10 years ago. Well over three million of our young people will receive college and high school degrees this year, almost twice as many as 10 years ago. In the nation as a whole, 95 percent of today's students will complete the eighth grade, 70 percent will graduate from high school, and almost one-fourth will graduate from college. All of these ratios are up substantially from just a few years ago.

A third force leading to new and expanded demands on our state and local governments has been the nation's ever-increasing industrialization and economic affluence. Since the early 1950s, for example, the country's total manufacturing capacity has doubled. Over the same 15 years, similar increases were registered by the nation's total output of goods and services and by the average income per person. As a result, family income in the United States today is almost half again as large as that of any other nation in the world and, of course, many times greater than the income of most countries.

This increased prosperity has afforded the American people endless opportunities for a comfortable and rewarding life. But it has also refined our tastes and increased our awareness and concern over the environment around us. With our new-found affluence we have, in many instances, become dissatisfied with the level and quality of public services and uncomfortable with some of the problems that at an earlier date were ignored. We now, for example, place a much higher priority on maintaining spacious and beautiful parks and open areas in our local communities. The larger public libraries, new halls for the performing arts, and increased number of museums that were once thought of as luxuries are now considered essential for the joy and enrichment of our people. And poverty, though in absolute terms less serious today than at any time in our nation's history, has aroused our social conscience and caused us to become committed to the goal of its complete and final elimination. All of these new desires and changing attitudes have placed increased pressure on our state and local governments for more and better services.

The growth in state and local government operations, however, reflects much more than our efforts to solve past problems and provide for previously latent desires. Though the nation's urbanization, industrialization, and prosperity offer unlimited promise and opportunity to our society, they have also created their own set of problems—problems that most often call for the attention of our state and local governments. Air and water pollution, for example, has become one of the more widespread and unwelcome offshoots of our highly concentrated, affluent society.

In addition, the nation's population shift from the downtown areas to the suburbs has caused many of our central cities to become blighted and rundown and at the same time has reduced the tax base necessary for restoring and maintaining them. Further, as we have concentrated more people into smaller spaces, such problems as crime and juvenile delin-quency, slum and ghetto housing, and social and civil unrest have become more acute. And finally, the rapidly increasing stock of automobiles—and the leisure time and income to en-joy them—has created traffic congestion problems that pose a challenge to the imagination and resources of our local offi-cials. The increasing speed of our jet airliners and the grad-ually slowing pace of our city transfer systems have in fact established a new law of transportation—the longer the dis-tance to be traveled, the shorter the time needed to cover it.

All of these forces, trends, and problems have combined to place the machinery of our state and local governments under tremendous pressure. Our efforts to improve the general qual-ity of environment around us—and to enhance and maintain our social, moral, and economic values—have in almost every case called for the governments closest to the people to take on larger and larger responsibilities. And with the nation's eco-nomic growth and urbanization quickening—and the list of social and public needs growing—there seems little likelihood that these responsibilities will diminish in the near future. There is, in fact, reason to believe that the role assumed by these units in satisfying the nation's most urgent needs will continue to increase in scope and in magnitude.

Thus it is regrettable that at the time most factors are point-ing toward expansion of state and local government responsi-bilities, other forces are at play that tend to diminish the effec-tiveness of these governments in performing their various ac-tivities. Many of our state and local governments, for instance, have not responded in full—or in some cases even in part—to the changing times and to the ever-growing demands being placed upon them. Even though many of their most pressing problems—air and water pollution, traffic control, urban transportation, police and fire protection, education—are areawide or regional in nature, often there is no single government unit to handle these problems, or even coordination among the many smaller units that attempt to handle them. The average metropolitan area has 87 different units of government, and some cities, such as Chicago and New York, have well over 1,000. One recent study has shown that the nation's 200 metropolitan areas are now governed by more than 18,000 governmental units. In addition there are more than 3,000 counties, about 17,000 townships, and almost 50,000 special districts—including school districts, road districts, park districts, and fire-fighting districts. All together there are more than 80,000 local governments in the United States doing a job that one source estimates could be done effectively by 16,000 units.

This fragmentation of our local governments has left few units large enough in population, area, or taxable resources to apply modern and efficient methods to their problems. A recent study by the Committee for Economic Development concludes that the minimum size for an effective unit of government is a population of about 50,000. Yet the average population of local jurisdictions is 2,500, and less than half the local units contain as many as 1,000 people. Moreover, the inefficiencies of such small sizes are further complicated by a government structure which at times calls for as many as 11 overlapping layers of government to perform the same or similar functions. It is surely evident that such fragmentation and duplication of effort among the lower levels of government is not conducive to efficient operations.

Even more regrettable, the federal government's policies and programs often tend to encourage and intensify these disjointed efforts. Over the years, the federal government's response to the nation's many social needs has been what one senator has called the "Washington reflex"—the tendency "to discover a problem and then to throw money at it, hoping that it will somehow go away." This rather spontaneous—and all too often ill-planned and uncoordinated—reaction to these problems has prompted the establishment of some 399 separate federal aid appropriations to the state and local governments, almost a ninefold increase over just five years ago. As would be expected, such a diversity of separate, and in many cases disorganized, efforts forces some cities to become involved with as many as 100 or more different federal programs in order to satisfy local needs. Such induced fragmentation by the federal government surely discourages consolidation and coordination at the local level and further compounds the already existing inefficiencies.

One final, and certainly not insignificant, factor contributing to the state and local government's reduced effectiveness is the generally widespread inability of these units to generate sufficient revenues. Through recent history, these levels of government have had to rely on sales and property taxes to meet their revenue needs. As both of these taxes generally have responded slower to overall economic growth than the needs and problems caused by this growth, most state and local authorities have faced the rather common dilemma of watching their spending outpace their income. The alternatives have been to increase taxes—which is politically distasteful, raise debt limits, or rely even more heavily on grants-in-aid from the federal government.

Although tax increases and the implementation of new taxes have certainly not been uncommon, this avenue has not been used frequently enough to close the revenue–expenditure gap. Thus, the state and local governments have been forced to float larger bond issues and to become more dependent on funds from Washington. As a result, state and local government debt has increased fourfold since 1950, reaching nearly $100 billion in 1965. Over the same period, total federal grants to state and local governments rose from about $2 billion to over $11 billion. For the coming year the administration has requested that these funds be expanded to $17 billion, thus providing about one-fifth of all the revenues received by the state and local governments. As most of these funds are tied to specific projects, the flexibility and initiative of the local authorities in responding to their communities' needs is often restricted. In many cases, this further limits the state and local governments' effectiveness in solving their local problems.

The challenges and opportunities facing the nation's state and local governments are infinite. Our society's growing commitment to improve the quality of its environment and eliminate some of man's oldest problems has created a whole new set of needs that demand public attention. We must, in effect, see that poverty is eliminated, pollution controlled, crime reduced, central cities revitalized, slums removed, and, in general, our overall environment improved. But we must see that all of these objectives are met in the most effective and efficient means possible—and without damaging the political and economic system that placed such ambitious goals within our reach.

If the most desirable solutions to these problems are to be developed, the nation's state and local governments—the governmental units that should be most responsive to the people —need to take much of the initiative. In a nation as diverse as ours, we cannot hope to formulate national policies which account for all the differences between regions and between states. We cannot hope to develop uniform programs that will solve all the nation's social problems with equal effectiveness regardless of local circumstances. We need instead to encourage local communities and states to respond to their own needs, to develop the flexible policies necessary for each unique problem. We need to develop the strong state and local governments required to counterbalance our strong federal government. Indeed, we need to develop the home rule that will continue to make our federalism viable and effective.

If the state and local governments are to develop such strength—and become fully effective in meeting their many responsibilities—they must become more receptive to change and to modernization. They need to make efforts to streamline their operations and to coordinate and consolidate their programs. As more and more of the nation's social problems extend across present jurisdictional boundaries, the governmental units necessary to encompass and solve these problems must be formulated. The need in many cases will be for regional cooperation, regional planning, and in effect, regional governments. If we do not wish to see the federal government assume more and more of the responsibilities that traditionally—and logically—have belonged to our state and local governments, we must develop the organization and machinery at these lower levels that are necessary to do the job ahead.

Much of the burden for reforming state and local governments must rest with our elected and appointed public officials. These are the people who are most involved with the present problems and who in many cases best understand the limits and the advantages of the current system. But if these officials are to respond in full to the current situation—and consolidate those units of government that need consolidation and coordinate the efforts of those units that need coordination—responsible citizens in all our communities must become actively involved in the reform process. It is the duty of every citizen to encourage and to assist state and local officials as they develop more efficient and effective ways of doing their job.

The business community, however, is in a particularly unique position to fulfill its responsibility in this process. Because of its experience in administration and management and organization and reorganization, the business community can and should be a primary force in bringing about the needed changes. It was with this goal in mind that the National Chamber recently established a program to develop a more generalized view of the modernization problem.

On a more specific basis, businessmen can help state and local authorities apply the same techniques to government operations that have long been used to improve the productivity of the private sector. They can point out operations and units that need to be consolidated for better overall efficiency. Through the use of such scientific management techniques as operations research and systems analysis, businessmen can advise government officials on what are the most efficient methods to solve their problems. Businessmen can also help public officials apply these same scientific techniques to government decisions, encourage them to expand their cost-effectiveness studies and, in general, help them develop a more analytical approach to their budget and financial responsibilities. In brief, businessmen can act as management consultants to their state and local governments, and perhaps initiate a management revolution in the public sector similar to the one that began several years ago in the private sector.

With respect to these suggestions, it is interesting that Postmaster General O'Brien proposed recently that the Post Office Department be converted into a nonprofit government corporation, so as to take advantage of more businesslike management techniques in its operation.

The business community can also offer guidance and leadership to the state and local governments in their efforts to increase revenues. If these units of government are to retain their most desirable characteristics—responsiveness, flexibility, and diversity—they must remain as independent as is feasible of federal grants and the controls that accompany these funds. Where possible, taxes should be levied by those governments that spend the money. The local citizen should be able to see his tax money at work—and know exactly what public services and public programs he is paying for and how much they are costing.

But if incomes are to match outflows, it is likely that more states and communities will need to evaluate their present tax systems and perhaps make substantial revisions. More effective use of the property tax through uniform assessments and wider application of user taxes may prove necessary. It is even possible that after careful studies some of the current taxes will need to be supplemented by new sources of revenues.

In the way of a summary, let me briefly restate some of my observations on this all-important area of public activity. Because of the many social and economic changes currently at play in our society, the nation's state and local governments are being placed under intense pressure to satisfy a growing list of new and different public needs. Their ability to meet these obligations, however, has often been diminished because of outdated structural and institutional arrangements. Government fragmentation and duplication have in many cases reduced their ability to respond in an effective and efficient manner to the demands placed upon them. This necessitates that some of the smallest government units be consolidated; or if this is impractical, greater coordination of local efforts must be achieved.

Businessmen can help facilitate this process by analyzing present government operations, and, with the aid of scientific management techniques, by offering suggestions on how more efficient approaches to various problems can be implemented. It is hoped that, after these changes have been made, substantial savings will be realized, thus perhaps reducing some of the financial pressure currently being placed on these units of government. But finally, if after the appropriate changes have been made, state and local governments still find their revenues inadequate, business leaders can help public officials make further utilization of current tax sources and, if necessary, help develop new tax sources. Through all these efforts our state and local governments should be better prepared to assume their proper role in our changing society.

*Wage–price guideposts have not been very
effective as a means of controlling
inflation. The guidepost concept should not
be used as a control, but should be
revitalized as a public educational tool.*

10

Prosperity's Challenge

Speech before the International Freedom Festival Luncheon, sponsored by the Economic Club of Detroit in cooperation with the Greater Detroit Board of Commerce, Detroit, Michigan, June 30, 1966.

Continued economic growth poses challenging problems for our free market system. It poses problems because we have reached the stage of our economic development where we must learn to control what we have been able to create. We must learn to manage our prosperity or suffer the consequences.

Our economy is currently in the midst of the longest peacetime expansion in our nation's history. Since the recession of early 1961, we have moved through a period of recovery to new highs of prosperity. The extent of our progress during the past five years can best be appreciated, perhaps, by use of a few statistics.

- Employment has risen from less than 67 million to almost 74 million.
- Unemployment has dropped from five million to about three-million.
- Output of goods and services has increased from an annual rate of $501 billion to a rate of $714 billion.
- Industry is operating at more than 90 percent of capacity, and both capacity and output are continuing to increase.

These gains constitute remarkable achievements. They are only slightly dimmed by the problem we now face in maintaining future growth without exposing ourselves to serious inflation.

An important factor in our rebound from the recession of 1961 has been the government's monetary and fiscal policies. The Kennedy administration turned at an early stage to a program of increased government spending, but more importantly, it recognized that changes were needed in the tax structure.

In August of 1962, President Kennedy described tax rates as "so high as to weaken the very essence of the progress of a free society—the incentive for additional return for additional effort." Later, before the Economic Club of New York, he referred to "the accumulated evidence . . . that our present tax system . . . exerts too heavy a drag on growth in peacetime —that it siphons out of the private economy too large a share of personal and business purchasing power—that it reduces the financial incentives for personal effort, investment, and risk-taking."

Congress, while not accepting all of Mr. Kennedy's proposals, did enact liberalized depreciation rules and investment tax credits. As a stimulus to business, however, these changes in the tax structure were partially offset by the dampening effect of the encounter between the administration and the steel industry over the 1962 price increase.

Lyndon Johnson, upon assuming the responsibilities of President, intensified the efforts to foster full utilization of the nation's resources. With unemployment continuing to hover close to 6 percent, the need was clear for a quick restoration of consumer and business confidence. The action taken was an $11 billion tax cut for individuals and consumers, which was passed by Congress early in 1964. This tax cut was followed by excise tax reductions and expansionary economic and social programs, such as Appalachia, the Job Corps, and the War on Poverty.

With the reduction in taxes and with more money coming into the economy, there was a revival of business and consumer confidence. The free market economy responded. Businessmen revised their investment plans and started expansion and modernization programs which, over the past two years, have increased capital outlays some 30 percent. This increase in private investments created new jobs and provided new opportunities for the unemployed. Consumers also caught the spirit of optimism and began to spend more.

The result has been a dramatic change in the economic situation. The economy is now working at the upper limit of its potential output, and the economic slack of five years ago has been replaced in many sectors by labor shortages and delays in deliveries. President Johnson has referred to the difficulties growing out of such a fully utilized economy as "the problems of prosperity."

Even though many people may disagree with the President's approach to these problems, there can be no doubt of his commitment to economic growth or of his desire to resolve the more recent economic problems.

So far, various economic tools have been used in an effort to curb inflationary trends. One was an increase in the Federal Reserve discount rate in December of 1965 and a subsequent tightening of the banking system's reserve position. Another move toward constraint was the reinstatement the following March of some previously reduced excise taxes. Still another was the acceleration of personal and corporate income tax payments, which went into effect in May of 1966. In addition, further restraint has resulted from the $6 billion increase in Social Security taxes, which became effective on January 1, 1966. These measures have withdrawn money from the private sector of our economy and are directionally restraining inflationary pressures.

The administration, however, is apparently not convinced that the monetary and fiscal tools which have helped bring the economy to full employment are sufficient to cope with the problems of prosperity. Thus, the government has expanded its efforts to include a set of discretionary and, to some degree, discriminatory selective controls. Of these selective controls, I am particularly concerned about the direction and potential impact of the wage–price guideposts.

The U.S. guideposts were originally conceived and spelled out in 1962 by the President's Council of Economic Advisers. At that time, the guideposts were viewed basically as a means of calling attention to the relationships that exist between productivity, wages, and prices. It was hoped that a discussion of these relationships would make business and labor leaders more alert to the impact of their private decisions on the public interest. For example, it was thought that if wage demands were excessive, an enlightened public opinion would bring pressure to bear, causing the unions and their leaders to moderate their demands and accept noninflationary wage increases. Likewise, it was believed that similar pressure would be brought to bear on price increases that did not seem to be justified by higher labor costs or increased demand. In this way, noninflationary economic growth could be realized.

From a look at the record, it seems that the original proponents of the guideposts had no thought that these concepts might eventually evolve into direct control of wages and prices. In fact, the voluntary nature of the guideposts was explicitly stressed in the 1962 Economic Report of the President: "Mandatory controls in peacetime over the outcome of wage negotiations and over individual price decisions are neither desirable in the American tradition nor practical in a diffuse and decentralized continental economy."

Recent developments, however, strongly suggest that many wage and price decisions are no longer completely free and independent. No longer, it seems, is the guidepost concept looked upon as simply an educational device. The 1964 Economic Report of the President spotlighted a formula for computing noninflationary wage gains. This formula included a specific number for guiding wage settlements and offered a set of rules for appraising the legitimacy of given price decisions.

Since then, the administration has seen fit to support its guidepost concept by direct participation, on select occasions, in the wage and price decision process. In September of 1965, the administration moved the steel industry's labor–management negotiations to Washington and with great dispatch initiated a settlement under the aegis of the guidepost principle. This was followed by a confrontation with aluminum in October, with copper in November, and then again with steel the following February. Each industry, in turn, was "persuaded" to withdraw price increases which the administration deemed to be outside the bounds of permissible guidepost decisions and thus contrary to the public interest.

This pattern of events has now extended over a sufficient period of time that we should be able to evaluate its effectiveness and reach a judgment as to the desirability of its future use. Although the guidepost approach certainly has had an influence on our economy, we should consider whether it poses serious risks and dangers in the future.

Many economists, both in business and in the academic world, have warned that the risks and dangers are present. It is their view that within the framework of timely monetary and fiscal policy, the efficiency of the competitive enterprise system is dependent on freely fluctuating prices which reflect existing supply–demand relationships. They point out that any arbitrary control of an individual product price results in distortion of the use of the product and leads toward enforced allocation. It is also their view that holding down the price of individual products does not prevent inflation. In fact, instead of solving the problem, controls usually magnify the distortions caused by inflation and seriously hinder the efficient operation of the market system.

Professor Milton Friedman of the University of Chicago offered a vivid description not long ago of the distortions that can stem from price controls. He compared an inflationary economy to a steam-heat furnace running full blast.

> Controlling the heat in one room by closing the radiators in that room simply makes other rooms still more overheated. Closing all radiators lets the pressure build up in the boiler and increases the danger that it will explode. Closing or opening individual radiators is a good way to adjust the relative amount of heat in different rooms; it is not a good way to correct for overfueling the furnace. Similarly, changes in individual prices are a good way to adjust to changes in the supply or demand of individual products; [but] preventing individual prices from rising is not a good way to correct for a general tendency of prices to rise.

In considering our problem of distortion, the copper market is a good case in point. The copper industry tried in November of 1965 to adjust prices to the then prevailing supply–demand situation. The administration did not believe the increase was justified, so by persuasive reasoning and use of the government stockpiles, it caused the companies that had advanced their prices from 36 cents to 38 cents a pound to rescind the increases. This rollback was required despite an established foreign price of 38 cents, which later rose even higher.

In order to maintain the controlled price, the administration introduced copper export controls and released large quantities of the metal from government stockpiles. The government arranged to import 100,000 tons of copper at the 36-cent price, but only after arranging a loan of $10 million under highly favorable terms to the exporting nation, which, according to one estimate, increased the effective price of the imported copper to about 41 cents. Finally, in order to stimulate expansion in the industry's domestic production facilities, the government, according to a recent magazine article, is now standing ready to buy copper on long-term contracts at as much as 40 cents per pound and then resell it at the 36-cent market price.

We now have an extremely complex price situation with U.S. produced copper at 36 cents, some imported copper costing 41 cents, but put on the U.S. market at 36 cents, the foreign free market as high as 80 cents, and the U.S. scrap market at about 55 cents. This has led the president of one copper company to charge that "the copper market has dissolved into utter chaos." And, needless to point out, the taxpayer and the economy are bearing the burden of the November reduction in the form of indirect subsidies to the industry and the less efficient operation of the copper market.

Additional objections to the guideposts have been raised because of the selective manner in which they are applied. So far, application of the guidepost concept has been limited almost exclusively to business. More precisely, perhaps, the concept has been limited to those industries over which the government holds a means of persuasion—the release of stockpiles, defense contracts, and import–export controls. In fact, though businessmen so far have cooperated with the administration's efforts to curb inflation and have observed in varying degrees the spirit of the guideposts, labor leaders have openly opposed the whole concept.

This past year and a half, for example, labor was able to negotiate wage increases ranging from 4.5 to 5 percent in such key places as the automobile and rubber industries and a 4 percent settlement in aluminum, all well above the 3.2 guideposts. Even more striking from a local standpoint was the California building trades settlement that gave labor a 6 percent annual wage increase for each of the following three years. Disregard of the guidepost principle was further demonstrated in the recent New York transit settlement and the New Jersey trades agreement. And only a couple of weeks ago the press announced that a special presidential board ignored the guideposts in recommending a 5 percent wage increase for airline employees.

These examples lend weight to the warnings and skepticism that have been raised as to the guideposts. Of even more concern is the possibility that they might evolve into more formal controls. In just four years, we have seen the guideposts change from educational guides to semiformal controls. Many observers now fear they may eventually become legally sanctioned by Congress and enforced on a formal basis.

Several proposals now pending in Congress attest to the possibility of such a development. Under these proposals, certain key industries would have to go through various reporting and hearing procedures before they could increase their prices. The government could recommend and presumably enforce "remedial" action where such was felt necessary. I hardly need point out the detrimental effect such legislation would have on our competitive enterprise system.

What, then, are the alternatives? What course of action should we as businessmen recommend that the government follow? How can we most effectively meet the challenge of prosperity?

There is no denying the fact that our economy, through the timely assistance of sound monetary and fiscal policies, is experiencing the longest period of peacetime expansion in our history. The record also shows, however, that the use of guideposts as a semiformal control has not been generally effective. In some cases, the guideposts might have been misapplied. In all cases, they have disrupted the free play of the marketplace.

recommendation (1)

I think we should urge, therefore, that the guidepost concept not be used as a control, but should be revitalized as a public educational tool—with the full support of the administration—so that the public understands and supports what is necessary to keep our economy competitive and healthy. As educational devices, economic factors can be used to call attention to the relationships that exist between productivity, wages, and prices. By this means, the public has a better method of evaluating the economic responsibility of the parties involved in wage bargaining. We should also urge that our government place greater reliance on the free market, within a framework of appropriate monetary and fiscal policies, as the best means of keeping our economy healthy and on a sound basis. In this context, it is also the public's responsibility, for its own benefit and for the national interest, to insist that the guidepost be used in its proper manner and thus minimize future distortions in the marketplace.

Over the short term, it is possible that the corrective actions already taken will be sufficient to cope with inflationary pressures. This is particularly true if government spending can be kept within bounds and if the war in Vietnam does not seriously strain our resources. For the long run, we should be better prepared to deal with the problems of prosperity. This calls for improving the monetary and fiscal tools with which we have already had some experience and considerable success. It calls for refining their use and making them more flexible and more adaptable to changing conditions.

With the uncertainties that lie ahead in an increasingly complex world, we can ill afford to experiment with concepts which are untried and of questionable value. If inflationary pressures should intensify, nondefense expenditures should be reduced and other restraining measures should be employed. To make such measures more effective and precise, it would be well for the government to consider the establishment of a highly qualified, nonpolitical commission to explore the advantages and disadvantages of the various monetary and fiscal controls available to the government. Such a study might significantly expand our knowledge about the impact of various fiscal and monetary controls on the economic problems we face under conditions of full employment. It might also reveal a way of removing politics from the administration of fiscal controls in the same way that politics was removed from monetary controls many years ago. Thus, both instruments of policy could be applied in a more timely and knowledgeable manner.

Should such a commission be organized, it would be desirable for business to participate actively. All too often businessmen are inclined to leave too much of the initiative to government—to stand aloof and then complain when we see government taking what we are sure is the wrong course. President Johnson, I am convinced, respects our role in the economy, and I would say it is our fault if we do not foster a better exchange of views with government.

Our free enterprise system has been remarkably successful in realizing the nation's needs and desires. Government can provide the kind of climate under which that system can continue to flourish. By each playing its proper role, but maintaining communications and continuing to exchange views, government and business can meet the challenge of prosperity.

*Today's businessman is increasingly
involved in the whole arena of social,
economic, and political problems.*

11

The Many Faces of Business

Speech before The Forum, Hollins College, Virginia, March 13, 1967.

Not long ago, Dr. Joyce Brothers, psychologist and nationally syndicated columnist, headlined her column with these words: "Mr. Executive: No One Wants Your Job." She went on to point out that today's college students—or at least a growing number of them—view business with disinterest and, in many cases, disfavor. As a result, Dr. Brothers claimed that many college students, particularly those who are most capable and most articulate, refuse to consider a career in business. She even referred to a recent college report which showed that the lower a student's academic standing, the more likely it was that the student would choose a career in business.

Although I believe Dr. Brothers overstated her point, verification of some of these statements is available. It has been reported, for example, that 14 percent of Harvard's 1964 graduating class entered business, compared with almost 40 percent five years earlier. A Louis Harris survey showed that only 12 percent of the 1966 college seniors actually preferred positions in business to other alternatives. Nearly twice this percentage found teaching more attractive and more than four times as many preferred professional careers.

Other polls have turned up similar results and have added further insult by revealing some of the reasons for this disenchantment. Some surveys, for example, have found that college students view the businessman as a money grabber, self-centered uncultured, dull, tightfisted, and narrow-minded. In addition, they see him as an individual who doesn't care for people, who ignores social problems, who preys upon the population, who exploits labor, and who is disinterested in religion. And finally, these students are moved to dismiss the businessman as little more than a selfish profiteer, a mindless right-winger, and a narrow organization man.

As I am sure you can understand, these reported trends and attitudes have, to put it mildly, upset the more thoughtful businessman. Until these polls were unveiled, he believed that the traditional feeling of respect and admiration between business and the college student was surely eternal. The businessman, in fact, believed that others viewed him as he viewed himself—as a practical, down-to-earth, hard-working, broadminded, progressive, interesting, and competitive free-enterpriser. Further, he believed that others, college students included, no doubt looked up to him as a self-sacrificing community leader, pillar of society, generous to a fault, great supporter of education, patron of the arts, and in short, the salt of the earth. Indeed, the businessman—in the pre-poll days—thought of himself as a happy mix between Plato, Gandhi, Churchill, and Batman.

It is evident that if the businessman is as virtuous as he thinks he is—or at least as he once thought he was—the college student has lost something in the interpretation. But it is even more evident that if the businessman is not the bore that the college student thinks he is, the communications between the executive suite and the college classroom must have been almost nonexistent. To be sure, if the real businessman lies somewhere between these two extremes—if he is neither as drab as students view him nor as noble as he views himself—better rapport and understanding between these two vital groups of society can and must be established.

Because of this conviction, one of my first actions upon accepting the presidency of the U.S. Chamber of Commerce was to lay out a program of college–business symposiums. These symposiums were to serve as a forum where business leaders and college students could discuss timely issues and become better acquainted with each other's thoughts and opinions. Our goal was to begin by conducting at least one symposium in every state in the nation. The state chambers would then be urged to expand and extend the program and keep it as one of their highest priority activities. So far, about 30 such symposiums have been conducted or scheduled and more are on the drawing board. It was hoped that these activities would do a great deal to establish better understanding between business executives and college students.

It was apparent, however, that increased contact and communications between businessmen and college students was only the first step in the process of repairing the damaged relationship between these two groups. This interaction of ideas would give lasting results only if businessmen were able to give satisfactory answers to the students' greatest concerns and anxieties. Business had to consider, for example, the meaningfulness of its functions and objectives in light of the nation's current economic and social values. Business had to evaluate the responsiveness of its operations to the needs and realities of modern-day America. Business had to study its personnel and promotional practices and see if the young person did in fact receive the challenge and satisfaction he wanted and deserved. And finally, the business community had to face head-on the question of whether business was, after all, an outdated and declining institution, a haven for conformists and guardians of the *status quo*.

Although I must at the outset concede that I am not an unbiased observer on the subject, I firmly believe that business has answered or is answering these questions and challenges to the satisfaction of most people. It can be shown, I feel, that today's businessmen—or at least a great portion of them—not only appreciate the nation's highest goals and ambitions, but also have in fact helped establish them and will be a leading force in helping to achieve them. Business has also demonstrated, or is in a position to demonstrate, that no other career offers the college graduate more challenge, more opportunity, or a greater avenue for service than a position in private enterprise. And finally, I believe that the business institution has shown itself to be as vital and as necessary to the welfare and progress of our society today as it has been at any time in our nation's history.

Let me just briefly discuss some of the reasons I have this confidence in the nation's commercial and industrial enterprises. One of the most commendable goals of our society today is the complete and final elimination of poverty from the national scene. Even though our nation's average standard of living is at unprecedented levels, we as a society have been committed to become the first nation in the history of man to provide all its people—including those at the bottom of the income ladder—the opportunity to earn a decent and respectable living.

The greatest single force in the reduction of poverty over the years has been the growth of the nation's economy. As the economy has expanded, business and industry have invested in new plants and equipment and in the development of new products. These investments have in turn created jobs and incomes for the American worker, and provided the poor—and the not-so-poor—the opportunity to raise their standards of living. Through this process, poverty declined three-fourths of the way toward total elimination between 1929 and 1962—and has declined an additional seven million persons over the past five years.

Business groups have also contributed to the antipoverty campaign through substantial efforts to eliminate racial prejudice in hiring—one of the great contributors to poverty. Businessmen have also developed programs for the education and training of the disadvantaged worker and the underprivileged young person. I happen to have been involved in two such projects.

In Newark, New Jersey, for example, my company and six others combined to help keep high school students from becoming dropouts. We organized a schedule where the potential—or in some cases, actual—dropout worked half a day at one of the participating companies and went to school the other half-day. We attempted to make his work sufficiently rewarding moneywise so that there was little incentive for him to give up school and try to find full-time work elsewhere. And of course we used every opportunity to encourage the students to stay in school and do their very best. It was particularly gratifying to us that some of these marginal students decided, after receiving their high school degree, that they would go on to college.

My company was also involved in a different type of program for students in New York City. There we had some of the high schools provide us with a list of their more capable students who were not planning to attend college. We then approached these students with the opportunity of participating in a special type of college education at New York University. The courses for this program were uniquely tailored by the school's officials for our program and, among other things, included such skills as typing and shorthand. The students were to attend these courses for a given length of time, with all their expenses, including lunches and transportation costs, to be paid by the participating companies. Upon successful completion of the established requirements, the student would receive a diploma and a job offer from one of the firms. If, however, the student preferred not to work for one of the participating companies, he or she could take the skills, training, and education now possessed, and go to work for some other organization. As you can see, business usually directs its antipoverty efforts more to making the poor self-supporting than public-supported. We believe our approach generally affords a longer-lasting and more rewarding solution to the problem.

Business has also merged national goals with corporate objectives in its international operations. The United States has long recognized that one of the surest avenues to world peace and international stability is to improve the economic welfare and to raise the standard of living of the underdeveloped countries. The most proven means of accomplishing this goal has been through foreign private investment in these countries—most of which has come from U.S. corporations. By helping to develop the resources of these poor nations, American business has created new national wealth and provided employment on a scale never before anticipated.

In still another area of national concern—cultural development—business is also deeply involved. Businessmen, surprisingly enough, are also dedicated to making the whole of life more enjoyable and rewarding and not just materially more satisfying. We, too, are interested in that which is aesthetic, creative, and beautiful.

Our efforts to foster the cultural stature of the nation have taken many forms. But perhaps the most tangible example has been the responsibility business has assumed in planning and financing the most recent round of new halls for the performing arts. These have included, among others, the Lincoln Center in New York, the Jones Hall in Houston, and the just-begun John F. Kennedy Center in Washington. Almost without exception, the principal supporters of these new cultural centers—in both money and leadership—have been businessmen and business-based private foundations. One study found that for the year 1964, more than 40 percent of all the direct contributions to the performing arts came from these two sources. The remaining contributions came almost entirely from individuals, many of whom were businessmen.

One additional area where business exercises notable social responsibility is its financial and moral support of the nation's colleges and universities. We as a nation have come to believe that the strength and worth of our society can be measured in large part by the educational attainment of our citizens. We have found that education is a tangible and profitable asset, the nation's first line of defense, and the individual's road to opportunity.

Many of us believe that privately supported schools are playing one of the most vital and necessary roles in meeting the nation's educational objectives. As the only institutions of higher learning that remain free from government directives, they are in a position to experiment, innovate, and provide strong academic leadership. Independence from central authority has made them a standard by which our public institutions can be appraised. For these reasons, I think it is important that our private colleges and universities be preserved and encouraged to grow.

One of the forces permitting this preservation and growth will be business contributions. My own company, for example, contributed more than $3 million last year to about 500 different schools, most of which were private institutions. Corporate donations to colleges have been increasing rapidly in recent years and in total reached $283 million last year. Additional hundreds of millions of dollars have been channeled into institutions of higher learning by business-based foundations, such as the Ford, Rockefeller, and Carnegie people.

These are but four areas—poverty, culture, international development, and education—where business involvement is substantial and where its activities extend beyond what are thought of as the traditional functions of business. The businessman's principal responsibility is and must continue to be to provide the American people with the highest standard of living in the world. But today's businessman is also increasingly involved in the whole arena of social, economic, and political problems. The challenges of managing an efficient and profitable business have been combined with the demands of public affairs and social welfare activities, which have been continually increasing in scope and magnitude. This has increased the boundaries of the businessman's activities to ever larger dimensions. His interests have been expanded to include such subjects as government–business relations, public affairs, investment analysis, international trade, union relations, public relations, social welfare, diversification, cultural development, and others. The challenge and diversity of his position have truly reached infinite proportions.

For the college students who wish to have their worth recognized, their efforts fairly judged, and their contributions rewarded—for those who want to make the most of their investment in education—business offers the natural outlet. But even more important, no other institution offers a greater opportunity for transforming idealism and independence into constructive action. No other career offers a greater opportunity to receive the satisfaction of making a contribution to society, of making the community and the nation a better place in which to live. And no other pursuit offers a greater intellectual challenge to the person with breadth of vision and depth of understanding.

The public should not be asked to endure unnecessary and unreasonable strikes. A new national labor policy should be established—one reflecting today's economic and social changes.

12

New Goals for National Labor Policy

Speech before the Executives Club of the Greater Boston Chamber of Commerce, Boston, Massachusetts, April 18, 1967.

In recent years, the American people have been made acutely aware of the inconvenience—and at times hardship—that can be caused by labor–management disputes. Some communities have seen their most essential services temporarily disrupted when nurses, firemen, teachers, and even doctors have staged walkouts. Other cities have experienced serious transportation problems when subway or taxi service was discontinued. Newspapers and television programs have been shut down or forced to improvise when key personnel walked off. And almost every major industry—airlines, electronics, petroleum, trucking, autos, railroads, and others—has suffered isolated or nationwide work stoppages.

These strikes, and others that are threatened, have caused widespread concern over the current procedures for handling labor–management conflicts. An increasing number of the American people believe that the some 25 percent of the nation's labor force represented by unions—and the even smaller percent that elect to strike in a given year—should not be allowed the power or the freedom to disrupt the nation's economy. In addition, concern is growing over the effect of certain unions' actions on individual freedom, employer rights, and the national interest.

Most recently some of these attitudes have been reflected in congressional proposals for resolving industrywide shutdowns. These proposals range from calling for longer back-to-work injunctions and compulsory arbitration to a suggestion that the government seize and operate any striking company until a settlement is reached. In almost every case, the idea is that when private bargaining breaks down, the government should step in and take over.

Any reasonable person would agree, I think, that the public should not be asked to endure unnecessary and unreasonable strikes, whether they be citywide or nationwide in scope. The nation's growing impatience with irresponsible demands and actions by either labor or management is understandable. But most of the current proposals for correcting recent or prospective situations do not seem satisfactory. These proposals in fact point more to resolving the strike once it has occurred rather than to reducing or eliminating some of the causes of strikes. They seem to offer little in the way of establishing a more workable and desirable relationship between labor and management—a relationship that protects the rights of the individual as well as improves the effectiveness of collective bargaining. Some of the proposals could even undermine or destroy the concepts of free individual choice and free collective bargaining—prospects that neither labor nor management finds attractive.

There are, however, areas of labor law reform that could remove many of the causes of our current problems. Thus, it is timely for the business community to reexamine some of the more important issues involved. We need, for example, to bring into sharper focus the rights of the individual, whether he is a union member or not. We also need a better understanding of the rights of employers, whether they have union workers or not. We need to evaluate the rules of collective bargaining and consider how they can be made more realistic and effective in meeting the nation's needs. We can then offer suggestions to Congress and to the American people on how labor policies and laws can be redefined or changed to more clearly reflect today's conditions.

I think we should accept as our general guides those laid out some years ago by Representative Graham Barden, a former chairman of the House Labor Committee. First, our proposals should avoid any antiunion intent; second, we should refrain from asking Congress for action that we know to be politically impossible; and third, our proposals must be those which the public can accept as fair and reasonable. In other words, we must analyze objectively the areas of dispute and attempt to view the problems through the eyes of those with whom we disagree. Only then will our efforts to develop a more realistic statement of labor policy and labor law prove productive.

Many of the present labor policies date from the National Labor Relations Act of 1935. The Wagner Act, as it was more commonly known, reflected the economic conditions of the Great Depression. One of the primary purposes of this law was to create an atmosphere that was less conducive to industrial strife and unrest. This was to be achieved by establishing a more equitable balance between the power of employees and the power of employers. With 20 percent of the labor force unemployed at the time, it was believed that the individual employee could not effectively bargain for better wages or better working conditions.

Between 1929 and 1935, the number of work stoppages had more than doubled and the number of workers involved in strikes had increased more than fourfold. About one out of four of these strikes was for recognition purposes, and the remainder resulted from economic disputes. The Wagner Act attempted to relieve both of these causes of strikes by providing for a method of union recognition and by encouraging the practice and procedure of collective bargaining.

The new law protected the right of individual employees to join together in labor organizations, if they so desired, and to bargain as a group with their employers. It further imposed upon the employer the obligation to bargain with his employees, if the employees had elected to band together. To administer the provisions of the Act, the National Labor Relations Board was created as a quasi-judicial body to settle questions of representation and to prevent unfair labor practices.

The Wagner Act did not, however, intend to establish a national policy of encouraging the unorganized to organize or, more specifically, of forcing employees into unions. It was not intended as a policy declaration of promoting unionism. In fact, Senator Wagner specifically stated in 1935 that the Act was not intended to "force or even counsel any employee to join any union if he prefers to deal directly and individually with his employer."

Any doubt as to the meaning of this statement of policy should have been removed by the Taft–Hartley Act in 1947. This Act was specifically designed to cure the problems that had been created by the NLRB's assumption that it should encourage, promote, and defend unions. The House Committee Report in 1947 criticized the NLRB for acting on the wrong assumption of what was intended by the Wagner Act.

Nevertheless, the National Labor Relations Board continues in its interpretation that the promotion of collective bargaining and the promotion of unions are synonymous. The NLRB still believes it has a congressional mandate to promote union-ism. This is illustrated by the recent statement of an official of the Board, who said the Congress in 1947 and 1959 merely changed the rules of the game—that the game itself remained one of promoting collective bargaining.

Even though the Board's conception of national policy may be a sincere one, it seems clear that the game was never one of encouraging employees to accept collective bargaining in lieu of individual bargaining. And if this was the game, it is doubly clear that Congress changed the game, not just the rules, in 1947. Nevertheless, this misconception of national policy by the NLRB does explain many of the controversial decisions of that agency and points up the need for labor law reform.

This need is emphasized by some of the Board's recent decisions on representation elections. As previously mentioned, one of the basic principles of our labor laws is the protection of the employee's freedom of choice—his freedom to determine whether to deal with an employer individually or collectively through a union. In 1947, Congress attempted to re-affirm this principle as an original policy of the nation's body of labor law. In Section 7 of the Taft–Hartley Act, Congress asserted that the individual had not only the right of joining a union but also the right of refraining from joining a union. And only after a majority of the workers involved had exercised this freedom in favor of acting collectively was the NLRB to designate a union as the appropriate bargaining unit.

Yet, many of the NLRB decisions run counter to this principle. The Board has, for example, established rules which, under some circumstances, require employers to bargain with unions without a secret vote by employees to determine whether the union actually represented them. On occasion it has also ordered employers to bargain with a union even though the union lost the representation election. And finally, in the Garwin Case, the Board imposed a union on the employer as a penalty, without giving the employees the opportunity to decide whether they wished such representation. These decisions, and many others like them, contradict our basic belief in individual freedom and point out the Board's misconceptions of what our nation's labor laws were intended to accomplish.

In many ways, the Board's attitude reflects the business and economic conditions that existed 30 years ago. In 1935, most unions were formed spontaneously by those employees directly involved. They were usually not influenced or directed by outside organizers or unions. It was for these reasons that Congress paid particular attention to protecting the employees' right of self-organization, a term still found in the policy statement of the law.

Today the nature of union organization is quite different. The typical organization effort is not a spontaneous movement of employees seeking a union. Instead, the typical effort today is a well-thought-out campaign that is directed by outside professional organizers. With the aid of such organizers and highly developed sales techniques, the employee is often subjected to misleading information and unusually strong union pressures.

Another change that has taken place has been the shift in power among the individual, the employer, and the union. The most serious threat today is not that the individual or union will be overpowered by the employer as it might have been in 1935; it is instead that the employer and individual will be overpowered by the union. This inequality of power is particularly evident in the case of a small company facing a large union. Such a company is often placed in the position where it is forced to accept a settlement that threatens its very existence.

Another area of change—and one requiring congressional guidance—revolves around the whole collective bargaining process. In 1935, Congress was interested primarily in getting the representatives of labor and management to the bargaining table and only secondarily interested in the problems that might develop inside the conference room. Today, employers are willing to meet at the bargaining table when their employees have chosen to act collectively. But once the bargaining process begins, both labor and management are on uncertain grounds. There are few congressional guidelines to direct the National Labor Relations Board in resolving bargaining conflicts. As the majority of the NLRB's cases today involve conflicts that occur inside the conference room, it is necessary for Congress to develop more definitive guides concerning the appropriate subjects for collective bargaining and the circumstances under which they should be considered.

Such guidelines should be premised on the need to improve the quality of the bargaining process rather than on increasing the number of issues to be considered. In recent years, negotiators have been required to consider a wider and wider range of subjects at the bargaining table. In addition to considering the basic issues of wages, hours, and working conditions, negotiators often have to settle such matters as Christmas bonuses, parking facilities, coffee breaks, and uniforms. Although some of these may be legitimate areas of concern, others have only tended to dilute the effectiveness of the bargaining process. We have even witnessed cases where the major issues were agreed upon well in advance, but strikes occurred because matters of minor concern to a small group could not be settled. In one well-publicized case, for example, the NLRB required labor and management to decide the price of coffee in an employees' cafeteria. Such extensions of the bargaining process detract from the effectiveness of negotiations.

A consideration of the appropriate limits and procedures of collective bargaining would perhaps also clear up the even more important issue of "business decision" bargaining. An increasing number of unions today are requesting a voice in matters that have traditionally been the exclusive responsibility of management. They are, for example, asking to be represented when such matters as the closing, sale, or moving of a plant are being considered. The union leaders argue that decisions on these matters affect the welfare of the company's work force and are thus legitimate areas for collective bargaining.

This view greatly oversimplifies the issue. Bargaining is desirable only where there is a reasonable chance for bargaining to be effective. Employers object to bargaining on basic business decisions. They must consider many factors such as stockholders' equity, size of market, financial arrangements, and transportation facilities. They are obligated to take into account the rights of many interested parties. They feel that bargaining on these issues is an invasion of management's prerogatives and may also jeopardize the rights of these other parties. In addition, many areas of decision bargaining involve confidential information that cannot be publicly discussed or released.

By the very nature of unions, the rules that govern their actions, and the pressures on their leaders, they can rarely make unbiased judgments on what is in the best interest of a given firm—which would also include the welfare of its employees. Obviously there are conflicting views on this issue. For this reason, congressional guidelines on the negotiation process should carefully consider what areas of bargaining can be productive and what areas are clearly and exclusively the authority and responsibility of either management or labor.

Congressional guidelines on the scope of bargaining would also need to consider exactly what constitutes "good faith" bargaining. The Board's interpretation of this concept has at times led to a bargaining process that discourages, rather than encourages, good faith. In one decision, it attempted to compel an employer to abandon bargaining strategy that was based on realism rather than on ritual. This decision seems to encourage both sides to take unnecessarily extreme positions—and then work toward a more reasonable compromise.

This is not to say that the interested parties should not engage in give-and-take bargaining or test an adversary by leading off with less than their best offer. But the NLRB should not interpret good faith bargaining as necessitating a prolonged negotiation period or an unrealistically large number of offers and concessions. To bargain in good faith certainly entails more than meeting standards as to a required length of time and a specified number of offers. The Taft–Hartley Act, for example, in 1947, stated that to bargain in good faith does not compel either party to agree to a proposal or require the making of a concession.

Management and labor should be allowed to bring more realism and maturity to the negotiation process. Such maturity and realism would surely improve the effectiveness and the image of this most important means for labor and management to settle disputes.

Finally, one other major policy area which needs careful consideration by Congress is the extent to which the labor laws should override other basic laws and rights. In particular, Congress should establish some policy on the extent to which such basics as property rights, the right of free speech, the right of privacy, and the right to protect confidential information should yield to labor law interpretation. Employers have long been concerned about various rules of the NLRB requiring an employer to allow his property to be used for the purpose of organizing a union which he prefers not to deal with, and in some cases, requiring an employer to allow these activities to take place on company time. The rules in this area are much too complex and extensive to discuss, but there is a wide range of situations where an employer is prohibited from exercising certain basic property rights. Examples of invasions of the right of privacy can also be cited. A case in point is the recent ruling of the NLRB that an organizing union is entitled to receive the names and home addresses of all employees, even over the objection of the employee. This is an invasion of the right of privacy in order to promote unionism.

These are only some of the areas that need to be considered as we attempt to develop a more realistic labor policy. Our economy and society have experienced fundamental changes since the Wagner Act was passed in 1935—and even since the passage of the Taft-Hartley Act in 1947. Many of the problems that the proponents of these Acts were trying to eliminate have long since been resolved. The balance of power between unions and management has been altered. Yet the National Labor Relations Board continues to reflect many of the attitudes that were prevalent 20 or 30 years ago. They have even extended the objectives of our labor laws from that of promoting collective bargaining to that of promoting unionization. They have accepted as their mandate the organization of the unorganized.

In order to bring our policy into closer agreement with the nation's needs and goals, we need to evaluate our basic objectives in the field of labor–management relations and determine what are the best judicial and administrative procedures for achieving these objectives. We need to reaffirm our belief that the individual has the right to organize or to refrain from being organized. And we need to develop realistic rules for guiding the collective bargaining process and for making it more effective.

If the necessary changes are to be made, Congress should move now to hold hearings on new labor legislation. It is time to evaluate our successes and failures in the field of labor–management relations and develop the laws required for the current and future environment. These laws should take into consideration the economic and social changes that have altered the relations between labor and management. They should consider the growing participation of government in all facets of this relationship. They should consider the public in general and our national interest. They should, in fact, consider all aspects of current and expected labor–management problems and foster concepts that are consistent with our free enterprise system.

The business community is willing to participate in the development of a more realistic labor policy. Some 40 trade associations, including the National Chamber, have banded together in a program for labor law reform. These associations have enlisted 150 labor law experts from throughout the United States to prepare proposed revisions in our laws and to document the reasons why such revisions are necessary. These proposals are realistic; they are reasonable; and they are not antiunion in nature. It is an excellent demonstration that business is approaching this problem in a responsible manner.

If we act wisely and effectively, we can help preserve the principles of our free enterprise system and help build a sounder base for labor–management relations. It is the responsibility of all businessmen to contribute to a realistic and appropriate national labor policy.

America stands on the threshold of dramatic economic progress. This progress, however, cannot be taken for granted, and we must avoid the pitfalls of the past.

13

A Look to the Future: Promise and Problems

Speech before the Los Angeles Chamber of Commerce, Los Angeles, California, September 30, 1966.

There was a time when Frank Lloyd Wright felt called upon to say that America was tilted and everything loose was sliding into California. There was also a time when a New York reporter came out on a visit, went for a drive on the Los Angeles freeways, and immediately wrote back: "I have seen the future, and it doesn't work." Today, however, such gibes have largely gone the way—or at least I hope they have—of jokes about Texas oilmen.

Instead, in the minds of more and more people throughout the country, California looms ever larger as a frontier of opportunity and a wonderland of innovation and imaginative achievement. Nowhere is it more evident than in the field of scientific and technological development. "It is in California," one observer has written, "that the marriage of science and industry has reached full flower."

For example, nearly 10 percent of the nation's scientists now call California their home. This concentration of scientific brainpower—considerably more than is found in any other state—is further enhanced by its high quality. Almost half of America's Nobel Prize winners now live in California, as do nearly one-fourth of the 740 members of the National Academy of Sciences.

Our nation's faith in California's scientific capabilities is shown by the number of government contracts awarded to the state's academic and industrial research centers. Between 1961 and 1965, these centers received nearly 40 percent of all federal research and development funds. Even more striking, the National Aeronautics and Space Administration, which we in Houston like to think of as a Texas organization, has committed almost half of its R and D expenditures to California institutions and businesses.

Los Angeles plays an active and vital role in this impressive scientific complex. A recent National Science Foundation survey shows that the scientific complex in the Los Angeles area has approximately 5,500 people engaged in research and development work. This is the third largest scientific concentration in the United States, bettered only by complexes in the New York City and Washington, D.C. areas.

Because of this area's commitment to science and technology, and because science and technology seem destined to play an important role in our future, I want to touch on some of the prospects and problems that lie ahead. As we approach the final third of the 20th century, we need to keep in mind not only the nation's achievements and its future potential, but also some barriers that could impede a realization of this potential. At the same time, we should keep in mind something Oliver Wendell Holmes once said: "Science is a good piece of furniture to have in your upper chamber provided common sense is on the ground floor."

By almost any measure, the 20th century has been a time of dynamic technological and economic change. At the turn of the century, the world speed record was 112 mph, set in 1893 by the Empire State Express. Today, our astronauts circle the globe at 18,000 mph—an increase of about 170 times. Even the least venturesome among us travel in jets at 600 mph and anticipate flying at 2,000 mph within the next decade. As though our schedules are not already sufficiently confused, such rapid speeds will often have us arriving at our destination earlier than the departure time.

Advances in communications have been equally dramatic. In 1900, it would have been difficult to be heard by an audience of even 5,000 people. Today, a person can reach 50 million or more in one evening. And in the near future, a development called holography, involving laser beam photography and communications satellites, may lead to world-wide, personal communication by three-dimensional television.

But probably the most significant development thus far in the 20th century has been the energy placed at man's disposal. When the 1900s began, the United States was consuming about 10 quadrillion Btu of energy per year. Last year we Americans used over 55 quadrillion Btu. Of even more staggering proportions is the power which can be realized from nuclear energy. One thermonuclear warhead could today release more energy than all the gunpowder and TNT exploded in all the wars of history. The multiplication factor per pound is about 50 million. We can only hope that man's wisdom and foresight will be sufficient to direct this energy toward the enhancement of man's welfare and not toward his ultimate and complete destruction.

These increases in speed and power have been accompanied by substantial, if not commensurate, advances in our nation's economy. Since the beginning of this century, America's real output of goods and services has increased 10 times and output per person has risen four times. The growth rate in the postwar period has been even more significant. In the relatively short period of 20 years, real output in the United States has doubled and real disposable income per person has grown about one-half.

Because of this rapid growth, the United States is by far the most prosperous nation in the world. With only 7 percent of the world's population and 6 percent of its land area, we currently produce about one-third of the world's total output.

With these past achievements as prologue, we are currently on the threshold of even more dramatic progress. The noted scientist and philosopher C. P. Snow has said that we are approaching "the biggest technological revolution men have known, far more intimate in the tone of our daily lives, and of course far quicker either than the agriculture transformation in Neolithic times or the early industrial revolution which made the present shape of the United States."

Anticipations of such rapid change are quite common and, for the most part, defensible. Today, there are about 400,000 scientists in the United States, more than triple the number of just 20 years ago. It is estimated in fact, that of all the scientists who ever lived, 90 percent are alive today. To support this large and growing number of scientists, our nation will commit $25 billion this year to research and development, some three times the amount spent just 10 years ago.

It is reasonable thus to expect this increasing emphasis on science and research to accelerate technological change. One recent study has shown this to be true. Before World War I the typical time lag between a scientific or engineering discovery and recognition of its commercial potential was about 30 years. Between the wars, this lag declined by about one-half, and in the post–World War II period, the time between a technical discovery and its application has been about nine years. Recent developments in the fields of electronic, computer, and space technologies as well as many others suggest this lag has been even further reduced in the past few years.

Technological innovation gives birth to new and better products and allows us to produce existing products more efficiently. Thus, acceleration of scientific development certainly bodes well for the future. Indeed, predictions about the approaching age of abundance, of leisure, and of a host of new and exotic products are enough to make us envy the next generation. Economists tell us that with even modest success, the nation's output in today's prices will exceed $1 trillion in 1975. Further, they see the classic income pyramid being inverted in the next decade as fewer people earn low incomes and an increasingly larger proportion of the population is concentrated in the $10,000-and-over income range.

The strength and vitality of the nation's economic system and our growing commitment to science and technology seem to make these favorable expectations well founded. Yet, we must not let our optimism make us careless and nearsighted, perhaps blinding us to the very pitfalls which could slow or even eliminate these bright prospects. It would certainly be foolish, and costly, to take unlimited progress for granted. As in the past, there are many impediments and barriers which must be overcome if the nation is to fully realize its great promise. I would like to mention just three of these possible problem areas.

One impediment to future progress could be a growing imbalance between the skills needed by our economy and those actually possessed by the labor force. The next generation will see change becoming not only more complex, but also occurring at an accelerated rate. It has been predicted that in 1975 some three-fourths of our labor force will be producing goods and services that have not yet been developed. Unless policymakers—at both public and private levels—demonstrate unusually keen foresight, our future economic and technological achievements could be tarnished by a large and growing reserve of unemployables.

The Bureau of Labor Statistics in a recent study found that the economy will need approximately four million additional skilled workers over the next decade, increasing their numbers by about one-fourth. With the continued introduction of automated and cybernated industrial processes and the increasing growth of our service industries, the nation's needs for highly educated professional and technical workers will expand at an even greater rate. In 1965, this group comprised 13 percent of all jobholders, compared to 9 percent in 1952. Between now and 1975, the nation's professional manpower requirements will continue to grow at about twice the rate of other labor needs.

Such an upgrading of the labor force is certainly a desirable, and in most respects inevitable, consequence of a highly developed technical economy. But if our educational and industrial institutions do not remain alert and responsive to these future needs, the effect could be serious dislocations of our human resources. Even today, some three million jobs remain unfilled because qualified people cannot be found. This situation exists though at the same time more than three million

Americans are seeking work. The possibility of our dynamic economy increasing this disparity between the types of skills needed and those available should not be discounted.

A second impediment to America realizing her full economic and technological potential is the federal government's poorly conceived policy toward capital investment. Our nation's unsurpassed standard of living is, more than anything else, a result of a highly productive economic system. Our productivity, in turn, reflects the willingness of American business to invest in new ideas, to expand facilities, and to modernize operations. As technological advance accelerates in the future, the welfare of our citizens will be even more dependent on business' readiness to spend on new plants and equipment.

Yet, in many respects the federal government seems to discourage, rather than stimulate, expenditures on plant modernization and investment in new technology. Our federal tax laws governing the depreciation life of productive plants and equipment are harmfully obsolete. They are based on a pattern set in the 1930s, when the pace of change in industry was much slower and when older equipment was adequate to keep up with competition.

Now, the administration is attempting to withdraw, at least temporarily, the most constructive, even though inadequate relief granted in recent years. Though the need for slowing the economy's pace is apparent, it is certainly questionable that rescinding the investment tax credit and accelerated depreciation allowance for industrial and commercial building is the most desirable means of achieving this objective.

The Committee for Economic Development recently presented a cogent argument for not only retaining such investment stimulants as the tax credit, but also for eventually reducing corporate profit tax rates. As a result of such a reduction, this group of scholars and businessmen contends physical investment would be stimulated, worker productivity increased, and economic welfare enhanced. In addition, as the rewards of increased industrial efficiency were passed on in lower prices, our international competitive position would show improvement, thus possibly resolving the balance-of-payments problem.

Other industrial nations of the West are far more realistic than the United States in their tax treatment of business, especially in tailoring their depreciation systems to modern needs. The Canadian system, for example, groups all depreciable property into 18 broad classes and applies across-the-board rates to each class. Each rate is set high enough to encourage replacement. This contrasts with our method of applying separate lines to thousands of facilities, all based on plant conditions of the 1930s. In some sections of Italy there is a 10-year tax exemption for new plants. The Netherlands provides fast write-offs of machinery costs for new plants in certain areas and exempts some new plants from property taxes for several years. Ireland exempts new industries from income taxes for a given number of years.

Hence, by international comparison, our tax system seems totally inadequate in stimulating plant and equipment investment. A whole new concept of business taxation in this country is one of the main requirements for our future progress.

A third possible barrier to our nation's progress is the attitude and posture of organized labor. Protected by laws and concepts formulated in the long-gone days of workers' relative weakness in economic affairs, union leaders are often reluctant to advance the age of technology. In fact, they have sometimes worked hard to hold it back.

Many labor leaders discourage and often prevent the introduction of automated methods. Their organizational power allows them to defy the public interest, even to the point of creating national emergencies. In the case of the recent airline strike, the union not only repudiated the efforts of a Presidential commission, the Labor Department, and finally the President, but dealt a most serious blow to thousands of fellow Americans. Many unions burden down industries with restrictive work practices, in spite of serious labor shortages. They have so disrupted the printing, railroad, construction, and urban transportation industries as to make them economic laggards and have knocked our ocean shipping industry out of world competition.

More so, I think, than any other requisite, it is imperative that unions play a more constructive role in building our nation's future. Technology is reversing the old order to the point where management and highly skilled labor are blending in the corporate structure—they enjoy similar prestige and pay—and still our labor law does not improve. The day is certainly overdue when organized labor realizes that its welfare depends entirely on the success and speed of our nation's technological progress.

Though the nation will no doubt face many problems in the future, these three I find particularly imminent and in need of immediate attention. If the nation's growth potential is to be realized, efforts must be made by business, government, and educators to achieve a better balance between the skills possessed by the labor force and those needed by the economy. At the same time, the federal government must take positive action to encourage increased capital investments. And finally, labor leaders must take a more enlightened view toward technological change and their public responsibility.

America's future does hold great promise. Our economic and technological progress has, in less than two centuries, lifted the United States from an agrarian society to the most powerful political and economic force in the world. Forces currently prevail which should allow us even greater progress in the future. But if the full promise of this progress is to be fulfilled we, as businessmen, must accept the responsibility of seeing that barriers impeding our nation's future success are removed. America will certainly be the better for our efforts.

Speech before the San Francisco Chamber of Commerce, San Francisco, California, September 8, 1966.